LANGUAGE MINORITY EDUCATION
IN THE UNITED STATES

LANGUAGE MINORITY EDUCATION IN THE UNITED STATES

Research, Policy and Practice

By

DIANE AUGUST, Ph.D.

Director, Education Division
Children's Defense Fund
Washington, D.C.

EUGENE E. GARCIA, Ph.D.

Professor of Education and Psychology
University of California, Santa Cruz
Santa Cruz, California

CHARLES C THOMAS • PUBLISHER
Springfield • Illinois • U.S.A.

Published and Distributed Throughout the World by

CHARLES C THOMAS • PUBLISHER

2600 South First Street

Springfield, Illinois 62794-9265

© *1988 by* CHARLES C THOMAS • PUBLISHER

ISBN 0-398-05482-7

Library of Congress Catalog Card Number: 88-8588

With THOMAS BOOKS *careful attention is given to all details of manufacturing
and design. It is the Publisher's desire to present books that are satisfactory as to their
physical qualities and artistic possibilities and appropriate for their particular use.*
THOMAS BOOKS *will be true to those laws of quality that assure a good name
and good will.*

Printed in the United States of America
Q-R-3

Library of Congress Cataloging in Publication Data

August, Diane
 Language minority education in the United
States: research, policy, and practice/by Diane August,
Eugene E. Garcia.
  p. cm.
 Bibliography: p.
 Includes index.
 ISBN 0-398-05482-7
 1.Education, Bilingual—United States. 2.Linguis-
tic minorities—Education—United States.3.English
language—Study and teaching—United States—Bilin-
gual method. 4.Education, Bilingual—Law and legis-
lation—United States. 5.Education and state—United
States.
I.Garcia, Eugene E. II.Title.
LC3731.A92 1988
371.97′0973—dc19   88-8588
                                                            CIP

PREFACE

THE AUTHORS decided to write this book after giving an invited workshop on the education of language minority students for the Society for Research in Child Development Summer Institute in 1985. Participants were researchers interested in social policy.

Our goal for the workshop was to help academics understand the linkage between research, policy, and practice. As academics ourselves, who are interested in this area, we knew that all too often researchers are removed from both the practice and policy arenas. Consequently, research often fails to contribute to improving practice or enhancing policy decisions.

To help with the workshop, we invited five presenters with substantive backgrounds in the education of language minority children who had also applied their knowledge to improving practice and policy. They were: James Lyons, Consultant for the National Association of Bilingual Education, with extensive experience contributing to federal and state legislation; Nancy Mendoza, Director of Bilingual Education for the state of Arizona, with main responsibility for implementing the 1984 Arizona Bilingual Education Act; Peter Roos, Attorney for Multicultural Education, Training and Advocacy, Inc., with 20 years experience litigating on behalf of language minority children; Kenji Hakuta, Professor of Education and Psychology at the University of California, Santa Cruz; and James Cummins, Associate Professor and Director of the Heritage Language Resources Unit at the Ontario Institute for Studies in Education, academics who have used their research findings to improve policy and practice.

The enthusiasm of the participants convinced us that we should write a small book that would provide policymakers, practitioners, and researchers with a broad perspective on the education of language minority students, bringing together information that is generally scattered throughout the literature on this population.

We used the presentations of our speakers and the reactions of participants as a springboard for our work and supplemented it with extensive research literature and document reviews and personal interviews with experts intimately involved in research, policy, and practice. The result is a volume that provides an overview of research and programs of significance to language minority students. It also includes an overview of national and state legislative and administrative policy, as well as judicial decisions and their related consequences for education of students. We attempt to address the research/policy/program interface in a manner which elucidates the recent trends in this emerging area of education.

It is our hope that this small volume will be useful for all those concerned with and committed to improving the quality of education for millions of language minority children residing in the United States.

D.A.
E.E.G.

ACKNOWLEDGMENTS

W E ESPECIALLY wish to thank the five presenters at the Society for Research in Child Development 1985 Summer Institute on the education of language minority students—James Cummins, Kenji Hakuta, James Lyons, Nancy Mendoza, and Peter Roos. Their presentations inspired us to write this book. We especially appreciate Nancy Mendoza who reviewed and revised the Arizona case study. We also thank the Society for Research in Child Development for making the workshop possible.

We are grateful to Lori Orum, Education Component Director of the National Council of La Raza, who contributed a portion of the federal initiatives chapter. As a policy analyst for La Raza she was intimately involved in the reauthorization of the 1984 Bilingual Education Act and was thus able to "bring the process to life."

We also wish to acknowledge the contributions of the following people: Dan Holt, Consultant with the California Bilingual Education Office, for providing the information necessary to write the California case study and for reviewing case study drafts. Julia Lara, Consultant with the Council of Chief State School Officers, for sharing with us information on state department of education policies for language minority students; Alex Stein, Consultant with the U.S. Department of Education Office of Bilingual Education and Language Minority Affairs, for reviewing and commenting on the federal initiatives chapter; Arturo Vargas, Policy Analyst at the National Council of La Raza, for providing information on the 1988 Bilingual Education Act reauthorization; and Conchita Biebrich for preparing the manuscript.

CONTENTS

LANGUAGE MINORITY EDUCATION IN THE UNITED STATES

Chapter 1

INTRODUCTION

LANGUAGE MINORITY STUDENT DEFINED

NOT SURPRISINGLY, as one searches for a comprehensive definition of "language minority student" a continuum of definitional
attempts unfolds. At one end of this continuum are general definitions
such as "the students who come from a home where English is not the
major language of communication." At the other end of this continuum
are the operational definitions common to the field of education ("students answered positively to questions concerning their use of two languages"; "students scored less than 25 percent on a standardized test of
English language proficiency"). Regardless of the definition adopted, it
is apparent that these students come in a variety of linguistic shapes and
forms. The language minority population of the United States is, by all
accounts, linguistically heterogeneous. Distinct dialect variations of
Spanish characterize one major subgroup of this population. Some
members of the Hispanic group are monolingual Spanish speakers,
others are monolingual English speakers; others are bilingual in Spanish
and English to some degree. Other non-English-speaking minority
groups in the U.S. are similarly linguistically heterogeneous. Moreover,
the language students from these groups speak does not remain static.
Not inconsequential is the related cultural attributes of this population
making these students not only linguistically distinct but also culturally
distinct. Describing the "typical" language minority student is therefore
highly problematic.

The term "language minority student" in this text suggests the acquisition of a language other than English. This definition includes the
following conditions:

3

1. Students are exposed "naturally" to the system of the non-English language as it is used in the form of social interaction, initially at home and possibly later in other social institutions. This condition requires a substantive non-English-speaking environment.
2. Students are able to comprehend and/or produce normal aspects of a language other than English. This condition implies normal language acquisition and function in a language other than English.
3. Students are later exposed "naturally" to the English language as it is used in the form of social interaction. This includes "natural" exposure in schooling contexts.

The preceding combined conditions define the present population of interest. It is clear from this definition that an attempt is made to include both the student's native and English linguistic environments. In sum, the language minority student is one: (a) who is characterized by substantive participation in a non-English-speaking social environment, (b) who has acquired the normal communicative abilities of that social environment, and (c) who is exposed to substantive English-speaking environments during the formal educational process.

Estimates of the number of language minority students have been compiled by the federal government on several occasions (O'Mally, 1981; Development Associates, 1984). These estimates differ because of the definition adopted for identifying these students, the particular measure utilized to obtain the estimate, and the statistical treatment utilized to generalize beyond the actual sample obtained. For example, O'Malley (1981) defined the language minority student population by utilizing a specific cutoff score on an English language proficiency test administered to a stratified sample of students. Development Associates (1984) estimated the population by utilizing reports from a stratified sample of local school districts. Therefore, estimates of language minority students have ranged between 1,300,000 (Development Associates, 1984) to 3,600,000 (O'Malley, 1981).

To provide additional information regarding this population, we will briefly turn to the comprehensive report by the National Center for Education Statistics (O'Malley et al., 1981), a follow-up analysis of the report (Waggoner, 1984) and a report by Development Associates (1984):

1. The total number of language minority children, ages 5-14, in 1976 approximated 2.52 million, with a drop to 2.39 million in 1980 and a projected gradual increase to 3.40 million in the year 2000 (Waggoner, 1984). In 1983, this population was more conser-

vatively estimated to be 1.29 million (Development Associates, 1984). Recall that this divergence in estimates reflects the procedures used to obtain language minority "counts" and estimates.

2. The majority of these children reside throughout the United States but with distinct geographical clustering. For example, about 62 percent of language minority children are found in Arizona, Colorado, California, New Mexico, and Texas (O'Malley, 1981; Development Associates, 1984; Waggoner, 1984).

3. Of the estimated number of language minority children in 1978, 72 percent were of Spanish language background, 22 percent other European languages, 5 percent Asians, and 1 percent American Indian. However, such distributions will change due to differential growth rates, and by the year 2000, the proportion of Spanish language background children is projected to be about 77 percent of the total (O'Malley, 1981). Estimates by Development Associates (1984) for students in grades K-6 indicate that 76 percent are Spanish language background; 8 percent Southeast Asian (Vietnamese, Cambodian, Hmong, etc.); 5 percent other European; 5 percent East Asian (Chinese, Korean, etc.); and 5 percent other (Arabic, Navaho, etc.).

4. For the national school districts sample utilized by Development Associates (1984), 17 percent of the total K-6 student population was estimated as language minority.

Regardless of differing estimates, a significant number of students from language backgrounds other than English are served by U.S. schools. Moreover, this population is expected to increase steadily in the future. The challenge these students present to U.S. educational institutions will continue to increase concomitantly.

THEORETICAL AND RESEARCH FOUNDATIONS

The disciplines of linguistics, psychology, sociology and anthropology have contributed significantly to our present understanding of language minority students. Researchers have studied bilingualism (Hakuta, 1985), second-language acquisition (McLaughlin, 1984), and academic-related programming (Wong-Fillmore and Valadez, 1985). Theories have been formulated to explain language and cognition (Cummins, 1985), second-language learning (Krashen, 1984) and bilingualism (Garcia, 1983).

The federal government through a number of initiatives has invested in research programs and evaluation projects related to language minority students. These resources and the scholarly interest which they have created provide an abundant and serious literature related to language minority populations.

Although it is impossible to do justice in this volume to the large literature presently available, the volume will synthesize significant research findings on bilingualism, second-language acquisition, language and cognition, instructional features, and program evaluation. The richness and diversity of the research findings will help to expose the complexity of language minority student education.

EDUCATIONAL PROGRAMS

For a school district staff with language minority students there are many possible program options: "transitional bilingual education," "maintenance bilingual education," "English as a Second Language" (ESL), "immersion," "sheltered English," and "submersion." Ultimately, staff will reject program labels and instead answer the following questions:

1. What are the native language (L1) and second-language (L2) characteristics of the students, families and community(ies) we serve?
2. What model of instruction is desired?:
   (a) How do we choose to utilize L1 and L2 **as mediums of instruction**?
   (b) How do we choose to handle the **instruction** of L1 and L2?
3. What is the nature of staff and resources necessary to implement the desired instruction?

School district staff have been creative in developing a wide range of language minority student programs. They have answered the above questions differentially for: (a) different language groups (Spanish, Vietnamese, Chinese, etc.); (b) different grade levels within a school; (c) different subgroups of language minority students within a classroom; and even different levels of language proficiency. The result has been a broad and at times perplexing variety of program models. This volume will address the current status of program service and promising instructional initiatives which are relevant to language minority students.

FEDERAL AND STATE POLICIES

The immediately preceding discussion has attempted to lay a foundation for understanding **who** the language minority student is and **how** that student has been served. This introductory discussion turns now to educational policy: first, federal legal and legislative initiatives, and second, "selected" state initiatives.

Federal Legal Initiatives

The 1974 United States Supreme Court decision in *Lau v. Nichols* (414 U.S. 563) is the landmark statement of the rights of language minority students indicating that limited-English-proficient students must be provided with language support:

> [T]here is no equality of treatment merely by providing students with the same facilities, textbooks, teachers, and curriculum: for students who do not understand English are effectively foreclosed from any meaningful education.

> Basic English skills are at the very core of what these public schools teach. Imposition of a requirement that, before a child can effectively participate in the education program he must already have acquired those basic skills is to make a mockery of public education. We know that those who do not understand English are certain to find their classroom experiences wholly incomprehensible and in no way meaningful.

The Fifth Circuit *Castañeda v. Pickard* (1981) court set three requirements which constitute an appropriate program for language minority students:

1. The program must be based on a sound educational theory.
2. The program must be "reasonably calculated to implement effectively" the chosen theory.
3. The program must produce results in a reasonable time.

The courts have also required appropriate action to overcome language barriers. "Measures which will actually overcome the problem," are called for by the *U.S. v. Texas* court (506 F. Supp. at 433), or "results indicating that the language barriers confronting students are actually being overcome" are mandated by the *Castañeda* court (648 F.2d at 1010). Therefore, local school districts and state education agencies have a burden to assess the effectiveness of special language programs on an ongoing basis. Other court decisions have delineated staff professional training attributes and the particular role of standardized tests.

Federal Legislative Initiatives

The United States Congress set a minimum standard for the education of language minority students in public educational institutions in its passage of Title VI of the Civil Rights Act of 1964 prohibiting discrimination by educational institutions on the basis of race, color, sex or national origin and by the subsequent Equal Educational Opportunity Act of 1974 (EEOA). The EEOA was an effort by Congress to specifically define what constitutes a denial of constitutionally guaranteed equal educational opportunity. The EEOA provides in part:

> No state shall deny equal educational opportunities to an individual on account of his or her race, color, sex, or national origin, by....
>
> The failure by an educational agency to take appropriate action to overcome language barriers that impede equal participation by students in its instructional programs. 20 U.S.C. § 1703 (f).

This statute does not mandate specific education treatment, but it does require public educational agencies to operate special programs to meet the language needs of their students.

The Congress of the United States on five occasions (1968, 1974, 1978, 1984 and 1988) has passed major legislation related to the education of language minority students. The Bilingual Education Act (BEA) of 1968 was intended as a demonstration program designed to meet the educational needs of low-income, limited-English-speaking children. Grants were awarded to local educational agencies, institutions of higher education, or regional research facilities to: (a) develop and operate bilingual educational programs, native history and culture programs, early childhood education programs, adult education programs, and programs to train bilingual aides; (b) make efforts to attract and retain as teachers, individuals from non-English-speaking backgrounds; and (c) establish cooperation between the home and the school.

Four major reauthorizations of the BEA have occurred since 1968—in 1974, 1978, 1984 and 1988. As a consequence of the 1974 amendments (Public Law 93-380), a bilingual education program was defined for the first time as "instruction given in, and study of English and, to the extent necessary to allow a child to progress effectively through the education system, the native language" (Schneider, 1976). The goal of bilingual education continued to be a transition to English rather than maintenance of the native language. Children no longer had to be low-income to participate. New programs were funded, including a graduate fellowship program for study in the field of training teachers for bilingual educational programs, and a program for the development, assessment, and dissemination of classroom materials.

In the Bilingual Education Amendments of 1978 (Public Law 95-561), program eligibility was expanded to include students with limited-English academic proficiency as well as students with limited-English-speaking ability. Parents were given a greater role in program planning and operation. Teachers were required to be proficient in both English and the native language of the children in the program. Grant recipients were required to demonstrate how they would continue the program when federal funds were withdrawn (Congressional Research Service, 1984).

The Bilingual Education Act of 1984 created new program options including special alternative instructional programs that do not require use of the child's native language. State and local agency program staff were required to collect data, identify the population served and describe program effectiveness. Two Evaluation Assistance centers were established. There was an increase in funds available for part C training and technical assistance.

In 1988 Congress again reauthorized the Bilingual Education Act. It is likely that English-only programs will receive additional funds.

Over one billion federal dollars have been appropriated through Title VII legislation for educational activities (program development, program implementation, professional training, and research) for language minority students. In addition, other congressional appropriations (e.g. Vocational Education, Chapter 1, etc.) provide funds for language minority students.

State Initiatives

Through state legislation in place in 1984-85, twelve states mandate special educational services for language minority students, twelve states permit these services and one state prohibits them. Twenty-six states have no legislation that directly addresses language minority students.

State program policy for language minority students can be characterized as follows:

1. Implementing instructional programs that allow or require instruction in a language other than English (22 states);
2. Establishing special qualifications for the certification of professional instructional staff (28 states);

3. Providing school districts supplementary funds in support of educational programs (17 states);
4. Mandating a cultural component (13 states); and
5. Requiring parental consent for enrollment of students (15 states).

The federal government contributes to state bilingual education programs through Title VII grants made to states. States use these funds for collecting, analyzing, and publishing data on the state's LEP population, developing and evaluating programs, providing and coordinating technical assistance, and training staff.

A recent survey of State departments of education indicates that many states report a need for training in methodology, for materials and additional staff, and staff and parent training. Major goals include improving the English proficiency of LEP students and bringing these students to the level of students in all-English classrooms.

SUMMARY

Language minority students have received considerable educational attention at the national, state, and local level. Over a billion dollars has been spent by the federal government for research, evaluation, professional training, support services, and educational program implementation. Some states have also assumed funding obligations and have enacted legislation which requires or permits specific educational programs for these students. Concomitantly, court decisions have addressed equal educational treatment for these students. The remainder of this volume will explore in more detail the research, policy and program forces that have emerged as significant. In doing so, we acknowledge that these are forces which are reshaping the character of many of our schools.

Chapter 2

THEORETICAL AND RESEARCH FOUNDATIONS

T HE STUDY OF language continues to expose more and more complex issues in theories of linguistics, cognition, and socialization. What was once a study of linguistic structure and/or learning has become today an interlocking study of linguistic, psychological, and social domains, each important in its own right, but together converging in broader attempts to construct and reconstruct the nature of language. It is this multidimensional phenomenon which confronts an educator when addressing the educational "transmission" and incorporation of knowledge. For the educator with language minority students as a constituency, the issue of language becomes critically significant.

Within the last few years, research in language acquisition has shifted from the study of one language (Brown, 1973; Gonzalez, 1970) to the comparative study of children from diverse linguistic societies (Bowerman, 1975; Braine, 1976) and to the study of children acquiring more than one language (Fantini, 1980; Garcia, 1983; McLaughlin, 1984; Hakuta, 1986; McLaughlin, 1985). This chapter introduces the theoretical and empirical knowledge bases related to an understanding of language acquisition. Of particular interest is the population of children for which multilingual acquisition is the norm. The present treatment of language acquisition will include a brief discussion of monolingual development and more extended discussion of bilingual acquisition and second-language acquisition.

LANGUAGE AQUISITION

Within the last few decades, interest in language has been intense and has consistently resulted in a multiplicity of methods, terms and, of

11

course, theories and research publications (Skinner, 1957; Chomsky, 1959). We will in no way attempt to do justice to this immense body of literature, but we will attempt to summarize and discuss major trends in this field inasmuch as they relate to the basic topic of interest here: bilingualism and second-language acquisition. For more detailed reviews of monolingual language acquisition, several other publications (some technical, others not as technical) are recommended: Menyuk (1971), Cazden (1972), Brown (1973), Lenneberg and Lenneberg (1975), Braine (1976), Bloom (1978), de Villiers and de Villiers (1978), and Stewart (1983). This initial discussion of the nature of language is necessary, since research and theory in this area has, as will be seen later, significantly affected research and theory development in areas of bilingual and second-language acquisition.

When considering the observation and documentation of language, it seems appropriate to conclude that "languages are composed of speech sounds, syllables, morphemes and sentences, and meaning is largely conveyed by the properties and particular use of these units" (Menyuk, 1971). Therefore, language can be seen as a regularized system. Native speakers of a language can make judgments concerning this regularity by considering whether or not any utterance makes "sense." Although the emphasis has been placed on languages' structural regularity, additional evidence (Hymes, 1974; Bates, 1976; Bloom, 1978) clearly indicates that structure cannot stand alone. That is, the meaning of an utterance is conveyed by both its formal structure and the specific environment in which it occurs. Therefore, for any verbal signal to make "sense," we must also consider the physical and social characteristics of the surrounding environment.

Moreover, particular physical characteristics of the utterance itself (the intonation, stress, and so on, of the utterance) are important. These characteristics become more and more significant during the study of early language acquisition when the structure of the speaker's utterance is limited, yet functioning of verbal communication is quite complex. In sum, language is best understood as any verbal signal where effect depends on its linguistic and physical character in conjunction with its social context.

BILINGUAL ACQUISITION

Relative to native monolingual acquisition research, little systematic investigation has been available regarding children who are acquiring more than one language, simultaneously, during the early part of their lives. However, recent work in this area has centered separately on the linguistic (Garcia and Gonzalez, 1984), cognitive (Cummins, 1979), and social/communicative aspects (Duran, 1981) of the bilingual. That is, research with young bilingual populations has concentrated independently on three areas: (a) the developmental nature of phonology, morphology and syntax; (b) related cognitive attributes of bilinguals; and (c) the social/discourse characteristics of the bilingual. This section reviews research in these areas with an attempt at highlighting similar and disparate theoretical conceptualizations and empirical findings generated by these separate research endeavors. A proposed framework for integrating these three distinct subareas of bilingual research which has critical educational implications is advanced.

Early Childhood Bilingualism Defined

Although it remains difficult to define any term to the satisfaction of the theoretician, researcher and educator, for our purposes the following definition is offered. The term "bilingualism" here suggests the acquisition of two languages during the first five to seven years of life. This definition includes the following conditions:

1. Children are able to **comprehend and produce** aspects (lexicon, morphology, and syntax) of each language.
2. Children **function "naturally" in the two languages** as they are used in the form of social interaction. This condition requires a substantive bilingual environment in the child's first three to seven years of life. In many cases this exposure comes from within a nuclear and extended family network, but this need not be the case (visitors, and extended visits to foreign countries are examples of alternative environments).
3. The **simultaneous character of development** must be apparent in both languages. This is contrasted with the case in which a native speaker of one language, who after mastering that one language, begins on a course of second-language acquisition.

It is the preceding combined conditions that define the present bilingual population of interest. It is clear from this definition that an attempt is made to include both the child's linguistic abilities in conjunction with the social environment during an important psychological "segment" of life (Garcia, 1983).

Linguistic Development

It does seem clear that a child can learn more than one linguistic form for communicative purposes in many societies throughout the world. Sorenson (1967) describes the acquisition of three to four languages by young children who live in the Northwest Amazon region of South America. In this Brazilian-Colombian border region, the Tukano tribal language serves as the *lingua franca*, but there continue to exist some 25 clearly distinguishable linguistic groups. European colleagues Skutnabb-Kangas (1975) and Baetens Beardsmore (1982) have provided expanded discussions regarding the international proliferation of multilingualism. In the United States, Skrabanek (1970) and Waggoner (1984) report that school-age Hispanic children in the United States continue to be bilingual with no indication that this phenomenon will be disrupted. Reported work by Ronjat (1913), Pavlovitch (1920), Smith (1935), and Geissler (1938) suggests this phenomenon is not of recent interest.*

One of the first systematic linguistic investigations of bilingualism in young children was reported by Leopold (1939, 1947, 1949a & b). This author set out to study the simultaneous acquisition of English and German in his own daughter. These initial descriptive reports indicate that as she was exposed simultaneously to both languages during infancy, she seemed to weld both languages into one system during initial language production periods. For instance, early language forms were characterized by free mixing. Language production during later periods seem to indicate that the use of English and German grammatical forms developed independently.

More recently, with respect to expressive development, Padilla and Liebman (1975) report a longitudinal linguistic analysis of Spanish-English acquisition in two 3-year-old bilingual children reared in Spanish and English bilingual environments. These researchers followed the model of Brown (1973) in recording linguistic interactions of children over a five-month period. Children were exposed to Spanish and English from parents, siblings and extended family members. By an analysis of several dependent linguistic variables (phonological, morphological, and syntactic characteristics) over this time period, they observed gains in both languages, although several English forms were in evidence while similar Spanish forms were not. They also report the differentiation of linguistic systems at phonological, lexical and syntactic levels. They conclude:

*See Garcia (1983) and Hakuta (1986) for more expanded reviews of early bilingualism research.

[T]he appropriate use of both languages even in mixed utterances was evident; that is, correct word order was preserved. For example, there were no occurrences of "raining esta" or " a es baby," but there was evidence for such utterances as "esta raining" and "es a baby." There was also an absence of the redundance of unnecessary words which might tend to confuse meaning. (P. 51.)

Garcia (1983) reports developmental data related to the acquisition of Spanish and English for Spanish-English bilingual preschoolers (3-4 years old) and the acquisition of English for a group of matched English-only speakers. Bilingual children came from home environments where parents spoke 20-40 percent of the time in English and 60-80 percent in Spanish. However, older siblings in the home spoke more (70%) English than Spanish. The results of that study can be summarized as follows: (a) acquisition of both Spanish and English was evident at complex morphological levels for Spanish/English four-year-old children; (b) for the bilingual children studied, English was more advanced based on the quantity and quality of obtained morphological instances of language productions; and (c) there was no quantitative or qualitative difference between Spanish/English bilingual children and matched English-only controls on English language morphological productions.

Huerta (1977) conducted a longitudinal analysis of a Spanish/ English, bilingual, two-year-old child. Spanish and English were equally used in the home by parents. She reports a similar pattern of continuous Spanish/English development, although identifiable stages appeared in which one language forged ahead of the other. Moreover, she reports the significant occurrence of mixed language utterances which made use of both Spanish and English vocabulary as well as Spanish and English morphology. In all such cases, these mixed linguistic utterances were well formed and communicative.

Garcia, Maez, and Gonzalez (1983), in a national study of bilingual children four, five, and six years of age, found regional differences in the relative occurrence of switched language utterances. That is, bilingual Spanish/English children from Texas, Arizona, Colorado and New Mexico showed higher (15%-20%) incidences of language switched utterances than children from California, Illinois, New York or Florida, especially at prekindergarten levels. These findings suggest that some children may very well develop an "interlanguage" in addition to the acquisition of two independent language systems later in development.

The above "developmental" linguistic findings can be capsulated succinctly but not without acknowledging their tentative nature:

1. The acquisition of two languages can be parallel but need not be. That is, the qualitative character of one language may lag behind, surge ahead, or develop equally with the other language.
2. The acquisition of two languages may very well result in an interlanguage, incorporating the attributes (lexicon, morphology and syntax) of both languages. But this need not be the case. Languages may develop independently.
3. The acquisition of two languages need not hamper, structurally, the acquisition of either language.

Intelligence, Cognition, and Bilingualism

A separate but significant research approach to the understanding of bilingualism and its effects has focused on the cognitive (intellectual) character of bilinguals. Based on correlational studies indicating a negative relationship between childhood bilingualism and performance on standardized tests of intelligence, a causal statement linking bilingualism to "depressed" intelligence was tempting and this negative conclusion characterized much early work (Darcy, 1953). Due to the myriad of methodological problems of studies investigating this type of relationship, any conclusions concerning bilingualism and intellectual functioning (as measured by standardized individual or group intelligence tests) are extremely tentative in nature (Darcy, 1963).

With general shift away from standardized measures of intelligence, the cognitive character of bilingual children has received attention. Leopold (1939) in one of the first investigations of bilingual acquisition reported a general cognitive plasticity for his young bilingual daughter. He suggested that linguistic flexibility (in the form of bilingualism) was positively related to a number of non-linguistic, cognitive tasks such as categorization, verbal signal discrimination, and creativity. Peal and Lambert (1962) in a summarization of their work with French/English bilinguals and English monolinguals suggested that the intellectual experience of acquiring two languages contributed to advantageous mental flexibility, superior concept formation, and a generally diversified set of mental abilities.

Feldman and Shen (1972), Ianco-Worall (1972), Carringer (1974), and Cummins and Gulatson (1975) provide relevant evidence regarding such flexibility. Feldman and Shen (1973) report differential responding between Spanish/English bilinguals and English monolinguals across three separate tasks reflecting Piagetian-like problem solving and metalinguistic awareness. These tasks required children to: (1) identify an object (a cup) after its shape had been altered (smashed); (2) label familiar objects with nonsense words ("Wugs"); and (3) switch labels of familiar objects ("glass" for "cup," "dog" for "cat," "sun" for "moon," etc.) and to use these switched labels in a sentence. Results indicated significantly increased flexibility for bilinguals. Ianco-Worral (1972) compared matched bilinguals (Afrikaans/English) and monolingual (either Afrikaans or English) on metalinguistic tasks requiring separation of word-sounds (/b/) and word-meanings (bee). Comparison of scores on these tasks indicated that bilinguals concentrated more on attaching meaning to words rather than sounds. Ben-Zeev's (1977) work with Hebrew-English bilingual children is also related to the metalinguistic abilities of these children. Subjects in these studies showed superiority in symbol substitution and verbal transformational tasks. Ben-Zeev summarizes: "Two strategies characterized the thinking patterns of the bilinguals in relation to verbal material: readiness to impute structure and readiness to reorganize" (p. 1017).

Recent theoretical attempts linking bilingualism to cognitive attributes have emerged. In an attempt to identify more specifically the relationship between cognition and bilingualism, Cummins (1979, 1981) has proposed an interactive theoretical proposition: that children who achieve "balanced proficiency" in two languages are cognitively enhanced in comparison with monolingual children, and that children who do not achieve balanced proficiency in two languages (but who are immersed in a bilingual environment) may be cognitively "different" and possibly "disadvantaged."

MacNab (1979) takes issue with this interactionist conceptualization on several grounds. First, the data to support the interactionist position are preliminary Canadian. Second, these same data have previously been criticized on subject-selection criteria. As MacNab indicates, it is likely that only high-achieving and highly intelligent children were selected for inclusion into bilingual education groupings. Therefore, cognitive advantages already existed prior to bilingual "instruction" and most likely contributed to the success of bilingual development, not vice versa. Moreover, successful subjects came from either middle or high socioeconomic strata where education was a premium and learning a second language was openly rewarded. Learning a second language under such conditions is quite different from one dictated by economic depression as well as social and psychological repression of a minority language and culture. In sum, it is not necessary to account for differences in bilingual (balanced or not) and monolingual cognitive performance on the basis of a cognitive advantaged-disadvantaged conceptualization. Instead, it remains possible that individual differences in intellectual functioning combined with the support or non-support of the social context for acquiring linguistic and academic skills are the factors for any specific differences in bilingual and monolingual performance on cognitive measures.

Another interesting example of research in this general area was reported by Lambert and Tucker (1972). This study attempted to assess whether bilinguals were more "flexible" in the special case of language learning. Specifically, they asked, "Can French-English bilinguals recognize and acquire (phonetically) a third language (Russian) more effectively than English monolinguals recognize and learn (phonetically) a second language (Russian)?" Their results indicated no significant advantage on this task for bilinguals. Yet, any advantage (or disadvantage) may very well be dependent on the levels of similarity and difference between the languages. This same conclusion may be appropriate for the above-mentioned studies relating bilingualism to specific cognitive tasks. That is, any cognitive flexibility may be associated with the particular task of interest. Future research should more clearly delineate this formulation.

Any detailed conclusions concerning the relationship between the bilingual character of children and cognitive functioning must continue to remain tentative (Diaz, 1983; Hakuta, 1985; McLaughlin, 1985). However, it is the case that:

1. Bilingual children have been found to score lower than monolingual children on standardized measures of cognitive development, intelligence and school achievement.
2. Bilingual children have been found to score higher on specific Piagetian, metalinguistic, concept formation and creative cognitive tasks.
3. "Balanced" bilinguals have outperformed monolinguals and "unbalanced" bilinguals on specific cognitive and metalinguistic tasks.

Social/Communicative Aspects of Bilingualism

As previously noted, language is a critical social repertoire. The linguistic component of any social interaction most often determines the general quality of that interaction (Hymes, 1974; Halliday, 1975; Bates, 1976; Shantz, 1977; Cole et al., 1978; Canale, 1983). In doing so, it carries special importance for the bilingual child where social tasks include language choice. Moreover, like other children who acquire the ability to differentially employ linguistic codes determined by social attributes of the speaking context (Phillips, 1972; Ervin-Tripp and Mitchell-Kernan, 1977), bilingual children face the task of multiple-code differentiation. Implicit in this discussion is the general notion that languages must not only be mastered in a structural sense and operate in conjunction with cognitive processes, they must be utilized as a social instrument.

The study of language acquisition in context is known as **pragmatics** (Bates, 1976). This approach demands that we think of the context of communication as involving information about the speaker, the listener, the speaker's goal in using a particular utterance, the information assumed to be true in a particular speech context, and the rules governing discourse. For example, in considering the conversational rules for discourse, three aspects of language may be considered important: (a) how the child establishes a topic, (b) maintains a topic, or (c) changes the topic across "turns" in a conversation. Adult speakers are generally adept at introducing a new topic into a conversation by using such conventional routines as "Let me tell you about X" or "You'll never guess what happened today" or "I want to talk about Y." Adults can also maintain this topic across many turns in a conversation, even when the other person participating is not particularly cooperative, as the following dialogue between a bilingual mother and a three-year-old shows:

> Mother — Okay, Maria, let's see what we can figure out about the shapes of these blocks.
> Maria — This one's yellow.
> Mother — Si, yellow is a color, but can you tell me what shape this block is?
> Maria — Todos son amarillos. (They are all yellow.)
> Mother — Si, but we want to talk about **shape**. Tu sabes como. (You know how?)
> Maria — (holding up a triangle) This one, this one, this one, es amarillo. (is yellow)

The mother in this dialogue introduced the topic clearly and maintained it by repeating the key word. The mother marked the topic, maintained the topic across turns, and "blended in" the turns so that the child's participation was recognized. The child in the dialogue has certainly not acquired the last of these abilities. She makes no reference at all to what the adult has just said. She does manage to maintain her own topic (color). The essential point of this example is that communication between mother and child is much more than utilizing appropriate language forms, or even having the cognitive prerequisites to generate symbolic speech. Instead, communication also requires social prerequisites related to language use.

Interest in these social contexts has generated studies both in bilingual mother-child, teacher-child and child-child interaction. Garcia (1983) reports an investigation of mother-child interaction including the description of Spanish/English use by children and adults (the children's mothers) in three different contexts: (a) preschool instruction periods, (b) preschool free-play periods, and (c) the home. These descriptions pointed out very consistently that children, in particular, were "choosing" to initiate an interaction in either Spanish or English as a function of the language in which the mother was using to initiate that interaction. A closer qualitative examination of the same mother and children interacting is reported by Garcia and Carrasco (1981). This analysis suggested that almost 90 percent of mother-child interactions were initiated by the mother, most often in Spanish. That is, mothers most often did not allow children to initiate. For that small number of instances in which children did initiate, the topic determined language choice. That is, "what" the child spoke about was highly correlated with the language in which he/she chose to speak.

The richest data on the bilingual children dealing with topic initiation comes from child-child interactions. Ginishi (1981), while investigating the use of Spanish and English among first-graders, concluded that the general language initiation rule for these students was: "Speak to the listener in his/her best language." Her analysis suggests that children when speaking with other children, first made a choice regarding language of initiation based on their previous language-use history with their fellow students. Zentella (1981) agrees that bilingual students do make these decisions. However, she found another discourse rule operating: "You can speak to me in either Spanish or English." Although Genishi's (1981) and Zentella's (1981) discourse rules differ, each observation suggests that bilingual students make use of their social and language-use history to construct guidelines related to discourse initiation. These studies suggest that particular sociolinguistic environments lead bilingual students to be aware of language-choice issues related to discourse initiation.

A comprehensive understanding of early childhood bilingualism must, therefore, take into consideration more than the linguistic nature of the bilingual or the child's cognitive attributes. It must consider the child's surrounding environment. Recent data tentatively suggest that social context will determine:

1. The specific social language use rules for each language;
2. The roles assigned to each language.

The Interactive Dimension

The linguistic, cognitive and social domains of the bilingual experience have been demonstrated as individually important in understanding the essence of the bilingual child. But, the interaction of these would seem to more clearly describe the ongoing developmental quality of this phenomenon. This interactive conclusion suggests the following:

1. The linguistic, cognitive and social character of the bilingual child are developing simultaneously.
2. Linguistic, cognitive and social development are interrelated. That is, cognitive processing factors may act to influence linguistic and social development. Linguistic development (the ability to operate within the structural aspects of language(s)) may act to influence social and potential cognitive functioning. In turn, the development of social competence influences directly the acquisition of linguistic and cognitive repertoires.

This interactive conceptualization is meant to reflect the interrelationship between linguistic, cognitive and social aspects of bilingual development often missing in educational programming for this population. Changes in each of these domains may be attributed to changes in other domains and, in turn, may further alter the qualitative character of the bilingual. It is recent linguistic and cognitive and social discourse data related to bilingualism that have transformed the phenomenon from a purely linguistic framework into one which requires an integrative conceptualization.

SECOND-LANGUAGE ACQUISITION

The study of second-language acquisition must be considered here due to its applicability, both theoretically and methodologically, to the issue of language minority education. This form of research has been concerned with those variables operating in the acquisition of a second language after the native language has been acquired. Investigations of young children undergoing the process of second-language acquisition have been relatively recent. Research in this area has borrowed extensively from the work in first-language acquisition. That is, the same linguistic features have been of interest within the same methodological framework. Specifically, the procedure for accumulating data on second-language acquisition has taken two forms: (a) samples of spontaneous speech of the individual are gathered in his second language during periods of early, middle, and late exposure to the second language; and (b) cross-sectional investigations of individuals exposed for varying amounts of time to the second language are undertaken. Typically, investigations of the second type make use of specific language-measurement instruments designed to maximize the probability of the occurrence of certain linguistic features.

McLaughlin (1985) traces the reported scholarly interest in second-language acquisition to the third millenium B.C. when Sumerian scholars received the task of translating their Arkadian conquerers' language into their own. Egyptian historical records indicate that by 1500 B.C. multilingual dictionaries were available. According to McLaughlin (1985), Jewish scholars, Egyptians and Jews received educational experiences in Greek and Jewish scholars developed the comparative study of Semitic and non-Semitic languages, the scholarly foundation for modern comparative linguistics.

Klein (1986) reports that Roman children were often exposed to Greek speaking caretakers and developed bilingual skills during early childhood. However, most second-language teaching during this period took the form of introducing and stressing the target language's grammatical features. After the fall of the Roman Empire, Latin continued to be a popular second language, and during the Renaissance it was learned for purposes of enhancing general thinking abilities. Instructional techniques favored an emphasis on the systematic understanding of grammatical structures.

As early as the seventeenth century, Richards and Rodgers (1986) report that critics of the prevalent grammar-translation method of second-language teaching began to receive serious attention. C. Mariel (1793-1856) suggested that child language acquisition was the appropriate model for second-language teaching. F. Gorcin (1831-1896) proposed an instructional technique based on children's use of language. He suggested that language be taught in meaningful context utilizing gestures and actions which normally accompany verbal interaction.

McLaughlin (1985), Lein (1986) and Richards and Rodgers (1986) provide incisive reviews of the development of theoretical and instructional contributions related to second-language acquisition. (These reviews contain a more extended discussion of second-language acquisition.) These authors agree that several themes characterize the historical treatment of this phenomenon with respect to language minority students. These themes include:

A. An interest in the relationship between first-language and second-language acquisition and input;
B. An understanding that the individual and social circumstances within which a second language is acquired can determine the course of second-language acquisition;
C. A concern for psychological/cognitive processes utilized during second-language acquisition.

The following discussion will explore these themes in recent research and theoretical contexts.

First- and Second-Language Acquisition

Learner's errors have been considered significant in providing an understanding regarding the strategies and processes the learner is employing during second-language acquisition (Corder, 1967). Dulay and Burt (1947b) studied the errors in the natural speech of 179 5- to 8-year-olds learning English as a second language. They classified errors as either related to first language ("interference" errors) or related to normal language development ("developmental" errors). Their analysis indicated that "interference" accounted for only 4.7 percent of the errors, while 87.1 percent of the errors were similar to those made by children learning English as a first language. They postulated that a universal "creative construction process" accounts for second-language acquisition. The process was creative because no one had modeled the type of sentences that children produce when acquiring a second language, and they suggested that innate mechanisms caused children to use certain strategies to organize linguistic input. Dulay and Burt did not claim that they could define the specific nature of the innate mechanisms. They did claim, however, that these mechanisms have certain definable characteristics that lead children to use a limited set of hypotheses to deal with the knowledge they are acquiring. The strategies parallel those identified for first-language acquisition.

Krashen (1981, 1984) has developed a conceptualization of second-language acquisition which considers as fundamental this innate creative construction process. His "natural order" hypothesis indicates that the acquisition of grammatical structures by the second-language learner proceeds in a predictable, "natural" order, independent of first-language experiences and/or proficiency. Such acquisition occurs unconsciously without the learner's concern for recognizing or utilizing structural rules. However, his "monitor" hypothesis suggests that conscious learning of a second language can occur when the learner has achieved a significant knowledge of structural rules and has the time to apply those rules in a second-language learning situation. He concludes, however, that conscious learning of a second language is not as efficient or functional as the natural acquisition of a second language.

However, other research has documented a distinct interrelationship between first language and second acquisition. Ervin-Tripp (1974) conducted a study of 31 English-speaking children between the ages of four and nine who were living in Geneva and were attending French schools. She found that the errors these children made in French (their second language) were a result of their application of the same strategies that they had used in acquiring the first language. Such strategies as overgeneralization, production simplification, and loss of sentence medial items, all predicted the kinds of errors that appeared. In overgeneralization, the American children acquiring French applied a subject-verb-object strategy to all sentences in French and thus systematically misunderstood French passives. In production simplification, they resisted using two forms if they felt both forms had the same meaning. Also, medial pronouns were less often imitated than initial or final pronouns. She believed that interference errors occurred only when the second-language learner was forced to generate sentences about semantically difficult material or concepts unfamiliar in the new culture.

Moreover, the strategies children use in acquiring a second language may change as they become more proficient in the second language. At the beginning of L2 acquisition, imitation plays an important role in the language learning. As children acquire more of the target language, they begin to use first-language acquisition strategies to analyze this input.

Hakuta (1974) demonstrated that a child being studied, through rote memorization, acquired segments of speech called prefabricated patterns. Examples of these prefabricated patterns are various allomorphs of the copula, the segment "do you" as employed in **do** questions, and the segment "how to" as embedded in **how** questions. These patterns are very useful in communication. The child used these patterns without understanding their structure but with knowledge of which particular situations call for what patterns in order to communicate in the target language.

Wong-Fillmore (1976) spent a year observing five Spanish-speaking children acquiring English naturally and she noticed the same phenomena. The first thing the children did was to figure out what was being said by observing the relationship between certain expressions and the situational context. They inferred the meaning of certain words which they began to use as "formulaic expressions." (These expressions were acquired and used as analyzed wholes.) The formulaic expressions became the raw material used by the children in order to figure out the structure of the language. Wong-Fillmore gave two examples of how children use first-language acquisition strategies to begin to analyze these expressions: "The first involves noticing how parts of expressions used by others vary in accordance with changes in the speech situation in which they occur. The second involves noticing which parts of the formulaic expressions are like other utterances in the speech of others" (Wong-Fillmore, 1976, p. 47). As the children figured out which formulas in their speech could be varied, they were able to "free" the constituents they contained and use them in productive speech.

In addition, at the beginning of L2 acquisition, children seem to depend much more on first-language transfer strategies. As learners acquire more of the second language, they depend less on these strategies and more on such strategies characteristic of first-language acquisition as overgeneralization (Tarone, 1979).

As McLaughlin (1985) has summarized, children acquiring a second language may depend initially on transfer from the first language and on imitation and rote memorization of the second language. In more practical terms, the less interaction a second learner has with native speakers, the more likely transfer from the first language to the second language will be observed. As the second language is acquired, many of the strategies that children use to acquire the second language seem to be the same as those used in first-language acquisition.

The Importance of Target-Language Input

It is apparent that target-language input provides children with the raw material necessary for language acquisition. In addition, the frequency and salience of forms in the input data influence the presence of these forms in the output. Hatch (1974) found that the frequency of morphemes in the input data appears to influence the sequential acquisition of these morphemes. For example, the order of acquisition of question words appear to parallel their frequency in what children heard.

She also noted that there is an interaction between frequency of forms and semantic importance. A form appearing frequently, though of low semantic importance, will be acquired later. Larsen-Freeman (1976) found that in-class teacher talk of ESL teachers showed a similar rank-order for frequency of morphemes as found in the learner output. Hakuta (1975) discovered that the auxiliary most often omitted by learners in utterances involving the catenative "gonna" was "are." He found such a construction less perceptually salient to the learner because of its absence. The auxiliary because of its absence in the input resulted in its omission in the learner's output.

These observations make researchers (Hatch, 1974; Larsen-Freeman, 1976; Hakuta, 1985) question whether the invariant order of morpheme acquisition (Dulay and Burt, 1974) is a reaction to the input to which the learner was exposed. The correspondence between input and output suggests that interaction between speakers might be important in structuring language output. Even Krashen (1981), a proponent of the natural order of grammatical acquisition, suggests in his "input" hypothesis that second-language learning is enhanced under conditions in which the learner is provided with input that contains "the next level of linguistic competence." Krashen (1981) identifies this enhancement strategy as "providing comprehensible input." Paradoxically, however, he cautions against any conscious strategy to provide "comprehensible input" and instead suggests natural interaction which focuses on meaning. Therefore, even though second-language learning may be enriched by providing "comprehensible input," any attempt to do so without the "natural" concern for conveying meaning could be linguistically disruptive.

Conversely, Keenan (1976) hypothesizes that the interactions from which syntactic structures develop are determined by the rules of discourse. As indicated earlier in this chapter, certain rules are generally followed in order to carry on a conversation. One must first get the attention of the conversational partner. The speaker then nominates a topic and develops it. Partners take turns. Topic clarification, shifting, avoidance, and interruption characterize interactions. Finally, the topic is terminated.

Adult-child conversations are systematically organized. Conversations follow the rules of discourse. As a consequence, the child acquiring another language learns aspects of communication from each conversation. In adult-child conversations the rules of discourse put both the child and the adult under certain constraints (Hatch, 1978; McLaughlin, 1985; Garcia, 1986). These constraints structure the interaction and consequently also the output. The child must first get the adult's attention. Once this is accomplished by gestures and verbalizations, the child must nominate a topic. The adult is also constrained by the rules of discourse, in that the response must be relevant. For the response to be relevant, the information about the topic must be shared by both child and adult. The adult's response usually clarifies the topic that has been nominated by labeling it or asking for more information about it. **What? Where? Whose? What color? How many? What is X doing? Can X verb? Is X verbing?** These are the kinds of questions the adults can use in response to the child's topic nomination and be relevant. The child's response in turn must also be relevant. As a result, there is a great deal of what, where, whose, who is verbing, etc. Hatch (1978) hypothesized that this accounted for the order of acquisition of these forms in previous studies. If the child is unable to say something relevant, he or she can just repeat what the adult has said but with the appropriate intonation. He or she will answer a question with rising intonation and a statement with falling intonation.

In summary, current research suggests that natural communication situations must be provided for second-language acquisition to occur. Irregardless of the differences in emphasis of the theories discussed above, recent theoretical propositions regarding second-language acquisition propose that through natural conversations the learner receives the necessary input and structures which promote second-language acquisition.

Social Factors Related to Second-Language Acquisition

There are sociocultural variables that contribute to a child's motivation to communicate in the target language. The attitude that the learner has towards members of the cultural group whose language he or she is learning influences language acquisition. Gardner and Lambert (1972) found that the positive attitude of English-speaking Canadians towards French-speaking Canadians led to high integrative motivation to learn French. Oller and colleagues (Oller, Hudson, and Liu, 1977; Chihara and Oller, 1978; Oller, Baca, and Vigil, 1978) investigated the relationship between Chinese, Japanese, and Mexican students' achievement in English with their attitude towards the foreign language group. Positive attitudes toward the target-language group corresponded to higher language proficiency.

Schumann (1976) found that children are more motivated to learn a second language if they do not perceive this learning process as alienation from their own culture. If a child belongs to a family whose integration pattern is preservation of the native language and culture rather than assimilation or acculturation, the child may be less motivated to acquire the second language. There may be less impetus for a cultural group to assimilate or acculturate if that group has its own community in the "foreign country," or if the duration of residence in the foreign country is short.

Not only is the individual's attitude toward the target culture important, but the relationship between the two cultures influences second-language acquisition. Schumann (1976) hypothesized that the greater the social distance between the cultures, the greater the difficulty the second-language learner will have in learning the target language, and conversely, the smaller the social distance, the better will be the language-learning situation. Social distance is determined in part by the relative status of two cultures. Two cultures that are politically, culturally, and technically equal in status have less social distance than two cultures whose relationship is characterized by dominance or subordination. In addition, there is less social distance if the cultures of the two groups are congruent.

A child, motivated to learn a second language, still needs certain social skills to facilitate his or her ability to establish and maintain contact with speakers of the target language. Wong-Fillmore (1976) and Wong-Fillmore et al. (1985) suggest that individual differences in the social skills of the child influence the rate of second-language acquisition. Second-language learners who seem most successful employ specific social strategies:

1. Join a group and act as if you understand what's going on even if you don't. The learners must initiate interactions and pretend to know what is going on. As a result, they will be included in the conversations and activities.

2. Give the impression with a few well-chosen words that you can speak the language. Children must be willing to use whatever language they have and, as a result, other children will keep trying to communicate with them.

3. Count on your friends for help. The acquisition of language depends on the participation of both the learner and someone who already speaks the language, the friend. The children's friends helped in several ways. They showed faith in the learner's ability to learn the language, and by including the learner in their activities they made a real effort to

understand what the learner was saying. They also provided the learner with natural linguistic input that he or she could understand.

Seliger (1977) has also demonstrated that high-input generators are the most successful L2 learners. High-input generators are learners who place themselves in situations in which they are exposed to the target language and are willing to use it for communication. Therefore, they receive the necessary input as well as the opportunity for practice.

In summary, children acquire a second language naturally. Although the underlying cognitive processes used by children in acquiring a second language may be similar in all children, social skills and the social climate do seem to influence directly and significantly second-language acquisition.

Psychological/Cognitive Factors

Theoretical alternatives with emphasis on linguistic and psychological attributes of second-language acquisition have been forwarded by Krashen (1981) and Cummins (1979, 1981). Krashen's (1981) suggestion that second-language learning is positively related to linguistic exposure that is **just beyond** the learner's present level of comprehension is based on a psycholinguistic interpretation of factors of significance to second-language acquisition. The degree to which linguistic input is "comprehensible" to the learner determines the acquisition rate of the second language. Moreover, "comprehensibility" is itself influenced by an "affective filter" (Krashen, 1981, 1982). This filter is characterized as related to psychosocial attributes of the learner and/or learning contexts such as the learner's anxiety level, motivation to learn a second language, and the learner's individual self-confidence.

Cummins (1981, 1984) has proposed a developmental interdependence hypothesis which implies the importance of cognitive attributes of the language process. More specifically, the level of L2 competence that a learner attains is related to the type of competence the learner has developed in L1. Therefore, native language acquisition plays a key role in L2 acquisition, in part because cognitive attributes related to the acquisition of L1 are of critical importance in acquiring L2. In short, L1 acquisition lays a strong cognitive foundation for the acquisition of L2. Furthermore, Cummins (1981) proposes that specific thresholds of linguistic competence in L1 and L2 for the second-language learner must be attained to avoid potentially negative cognitive deficits. Alternatively, if these thresholds in L1 and L2 are reached, potentially beneficial cognitive attributes are a by-product.

Seliger (1984) and McLaughlin (1985) have proposed two different types of processes in acquiring a second language. One such process calls for the learner to formulate hypotheses and revise those hypotheses on the basis of language-specific cognitive "strategies." These "strategies" are considered universal and likely based on innate language-specific cognitive mechanisms (McLaughlin, 1985). These processes include such "strategies" as overgeneralization, simplification, and hypothesis testing. A second type of process assists learners in meeting the engagement demands of a particular situation. These "tactics" are chosen deliberately to overcome temporary and immediate obstacles to learning a task. Second-language learners may choose to learn the grammar, seek out native speakers, memorize vocabulary items, etc. (Seliger, 1984). In each case, "strategies" and "tactics" are viewed as cognitive mechanisms which assist the learner in the acquisition of the second language.

Hakuta (1985) likens second-language learning to a problem-solving task. The learner will use numerous strategies, hunches, hypotheses and related cognitive devices to solve the problem. This might include knowledge-related symbolic perceptual representation, organization, processing and utilization of such knowledge under differing circumstances to achieve different goals. Significantly, according to Hakuta (1985), the learner can transfer all the cognitive knowledge related to L1 to solving his L2 learning problem. The learner, having determined that language is symbolic, that it is made up of phonology, morphology and syntax, that it must be communicative, and that it must be structured around certain discourse rules, can rely on such information and related cognitive mechanisms for successfully addressing second-language learning. Therefore, cognitive prerequisites related to the understanding of language and its use acquired through the native language acquisition process may become key during second-language acquisition.

From the above review of second-language acquisition theory and research, "second-language" acquisition:

A. Has been characterized as **related** and **not related** to acquisition of L1 linguistic structures;

B. Has been related to specific rules of discourse;

C. May be influenced by the motivation to learn a second language;

D. Has been related to social factors;

E. Has been related to basic cognitive mechanism which are either universal, specific to a situation and/or components of native-language acquisition.

Hammerly (1985) has also suggested that it is useful to indicate what second-language acquisition is **not**:

A. An intellectual exercise involving the understanding and memorization of grammar;
B. Translation;
C. Memorization of sentences;
D. Mechanical conditioning; and/or
E. Applying abstract rules.

Our understanding of second-language acquisition requires cognizance of similar interrelationships identified earlier in this chapter when discussing the nature of bilingualism. Each phenomenon has been "diagnosed" as dependent on L1-L2 cross-linguistic effects in combination with the social aspects of language use and the psychological/ cognitive processes which serve to organize and guide learning. Certain theoretical emphases and contradictions combined with empirical emphases and contradictions discussed in this chapter continue to remind us that our understanding of second-language acquisition remains incomplete. This is not to suggest that little is known. The above discussion has presented a large body of research and various sophisticated conceptualization (theories) to guide our understanding of this phenomenon. However, theory and research related to second-language acquisition is far from complete.

THE NATURE OF SECOND-LANGUAGE ACQUISITION AS IT RELATES TO SCHOOLING

Unfortunately, education often considers language as a single, simple, unitary skill. However, recent conceptualizations of language indicate that language is not a unitary skill but rather a complex configuration of abilities. Most importantly, it seems that language used for conventional purposes is quite different from language used for school learning, and that the former develops earlier than the latter (Hakuta and Snow, 1986).

In the context of language minority education, this means that children become conversationally fluent in English before they develop the ability to actually use English in academic situations. Language minority educational programs are often criticized for keeping students too long, even after their English is adequate. English skill judged as "adequate" in an informal conversation, or even on a simple test, may not mean that the child's skills are adequate for understanding a teacher's explanation, for reading a textbook, or for writing a composition. Research tells us that conversational adequacy is not the appropriate criterion for mainstreaming students.

Hakuta and Snow (1986) and Wong-Fillmore and Valadez (1985) recommended that one major goal of language minority education should be the development of **the full repertoire of linguistic skills in English**, in preparation for participation in mainstream classes.

The Relationship of the Two Languages in the Curriculum

A major argument against the use of the native language has been that it does not develop English rapidly enough when it emphasizes the native language. However, the major premise of this argument—that the time spent in the classroom using the native language is wasted or lost—is overwhelmingly rejected by research. First, a strong native language foundation acts as a support in the learning of English, making it easier and faster. Second, most of the learning that goes on in the native language transfers readily to English. This is also true for content areas like math, science, and social studies. The child who already understands why "tres por ocho es igual a cuatro por seis" will not need to be taught such number equivalences again in English. Similarly, the child who knows how to write a topic sentence or look up a word in the dictionary in Portuguese or Chinese will have these skills available for use in the English classroom.

The implication of this finding is that time spent working and studying in the native language in bilingual classrooms is not time lost in developing the skills needed for school success. Becoming fluent in a second language does not necessarily mean losing the first language, nor does maintenance of the first language necessarily retard the development of the second language.

The Relationship of Language and General Mental Functioning

There exists a persistent belief that for minority children, bilingualism promotes the retardation of cognitive development. This belief is founded on some early attempts to explain why immigrants from southern and eastern Europe were performing poorly on IQ tests. However, current research shows that there is no such thing as retardation caused by bilingualism; if anything, the development of a second language can have positive effects on thinking skills. The advantage of bilingual children over monolingual children in cognitive flexibility has been shown in a number of different studies, particularly in contexts of additive bilingualism where the second language is added while the native language is maintained. These findings suggest that there is no cognitive cost to the development of bilingualism in children, and very possibly, bilingualism brings with it the added bonus of the enhancement of children's thinking skills.

The Differences Between Individual Children

Research cautions against attempting to formulate policy based on the observation of a limited number of children. There are, to be sure, documented cases of children who rapidly acquire a second language. However, the research shows these children to be the exception rather than the rule. There are tremendous variations across different children in the rate of which they learn the second language, and the process is not as painless as one would want to believe. The variation is due to a multitude of factors, including cultural background, the strength of the native language, home language environment, personality, attitude, and aptitude for learning languages.

Language minority education programs should have the flexibility to adjust to these large individual and cultural variations. Furthermore, educators should develop the expectation that it is not abnormal for some students to need bilingual instruction for relatively long periods of time, whereas others for whom all the individual and cultural factors support second-language learning may exit from special programs quite quickly.

The Optimal Age for Second Language Acquisition

Many people believe that only children can learn a second language quickly and easily, and that if children have not mastered the second language by early school years they never will. This belief has been responsible for a sense of urgency in introducing English to non-English-speaking children and for worries about postponing children's exit from bilingual programs.

However, the belief that children are fast and effortless second-language learners has no basis in fact. Teenagers and adults are much more efficient learners than elementary school children, and fourth to seventh graders learn more quickly than first to third graders. Research in Canada has shown that one year of immersion in the second-language classroom environment at seventh grade is worth three years' immersion starting at first grade (Hakuta, 1985). Especially for primary grade children, it is important to realize that second-language learning is likely to be a very slow process; but also that it can still be successful if started much later than age five or six.

Programs should be designed with the expectation that young school-age children learn second languages rather slowly, and will need several years of learning before their English is as good as that of children who have been speaking it since birth. It should be recognized that starting to speak English even as late as high school is no barrier to learning to speak it very well.

Literacy

Perhaps the major task of schools is teaching children to read. Many factors contribute to children's being good or poor readers as documented in the recent report of the Commission on Reading, *Becoming a Nation of Readers* (1986). One source of help to children's reading is the home; home is where children have access to time alone with adults, where literacy is modeled, displayed and valued and where parents' attitudes emphasize learning and school achievement. This type of environment typically produces children who have little difficulty learning to read. For children whose homes do not provide this kind of support to literacy, learning to read is a difficult task and one which can much better be started in the home language — the language the child knows best. Once the basic principles of reading are mastered in the home language, reading skills transfer quickly and easily to a second language.

Language minority education programs should concentrate on providing literacy skills in the home language, especially for those children whose parents have little education and poor literacy skills. The introduction of reading in English can be safely and efficiently postponed until after reading in the home language has been mastered. Reading achievement in English will be higher and will be attained in less time if reading is taught first in the home language.

Social Interactional Factors in Second-Language Acquisition

Obviously, having the opportunity to talk to a native speaker of English can only help in learning English. A criticism often leveled at bilingual programs is that they isolate non-English-speaking children from the English speakers who are their friends and who should be helping them learn English.

It is not the case, though, that merely playing with other children contributes much to the kind of language skills needed for school success. Young children can play, and have fun, and even "talk" together with rather little solid knowledge of each other's language. Learning the English language skills needed for school success requires much more, for most children, than just the ability to find some English-speaking playmates.

Children, like adults, only interact with people they like or admire. If non-English-speaking children in mainstream classrooms come from groups that are negatively stereotyped by the English speakers, they will not easily find English-speaking playmates. A major factor in giving minority children access to social interactions with English-speaking peers is upgrading the status of the minority group in the eyes of the majority (Cummins, 1986).

Social interaction with speakers can contribute to children's learning English. But just putting minority children in mainstream classrooms does not ensure interaction. Such submersion in mainstream classrooms is most likely to result in rapid stereotyped minority groups for children who have strong language literacy, and school-relevant skills in their native language. Other children need programs which emphasize the instructional use of the native language (Cummins, 1981, 1986).

GENERAL IMPLICATIONS FOR EDUCATION

The previous discussions of bilingual acquisition and second-language acquisition have attempted to highlight important data and theory which serve to provide an understanding of these phenomenon. This same data and theory, however, have influenced the educational treatment of language minority students. As indicated previously, the knowledge base in this area continues to expand, but is in no way to be considered complete or overly comprehensive. In addition, it would be an error to conclude that the data and theory that has emerged has been a primary factor in determining the educational treatment of language minority students. (In upcoming sections which review educational policy and programs, other factors will be discussed.) However, it does seem appropriate to identify in the present discussion possible program and policy implications derived from research and theory as highlighted by our own discussion and that of Hakuta and Snow (1986):

A. One major goal of language minority education should be the development of the full repertoire of linguistic skills in English, in preparation for participation in mainstream classes.

B. Time spent learning in the native language is not time lost in developing English. Children can become fluent in a second language without losing the first language, and can maintain the first language without retarding the development of the second language.

C. There is no cognitive cost to the development of bilingualism in children; very possibly, bilingualism enhances children's thinking skills.

D. Language minority education programs should have the flexibility of adjusting large individual and cultural differences among children. Furthermore, educators should develop the expectation that it is not abnormal for some students to need instruction in two languages for relatively long periods of time.

E. Educators should expect that young children will take a minimum of several years to learn a second language to a level like that of a native speaker. At the same time, they should not have lower expectations of older learners, who can typically learn languages quite quickly, and often end up speaking them just as younger learners.

F. Particularly for children who on other grounds are at risk for reading failure, reading should be taught in the native language. Reading skills acquired in the native language will transfer readily and quickly to English and will result in higher ultimate reading achievement in English.

G. A major problem for minority group children is that young English-speaking children share the negative stereotypes of their parents and the society at large. Any action that upgrades the status of the minority child and his language contributes to the child's opportunities for friendship with native English-speaking children.

In summary, theoretical (and, to some extent, empirical research) support can be identified for educational interventions which choose to utilize language in a variety of distinct ways within an educational program for language minority students. It seems necessary to conclude that the present state of research and theory with respect to the language and the education of language minority students does allow for some specific conclusions. Of course, we would recommend that educational professionals, in their quest to intervene for the betterment of language minority students, carefully scrutinize relevant theory and research and utilize that analysis to design, implement and evaluate interventions of significance to their particular educational circumstances. It is fair to request that such designers and implementors provide a clear theoretical and empirical and research foundation, one which can in turn receive the necessary careful scrutiny.

Chapter 3

EDUCATIONAL PROGRAMS

INSTRUCTIONAL MODELS

EDUCATIONAL programs for language minority students have taken on various forms.* The following discussion identifies instructional variables that have characterized education programs serving language minority students. Although programs that serve language minority students have the same goal of helping children acquire the English proficiency necessary to succeed in school, they differ in the manner in which they incorporate the native language of the student.

Lambert (1967), Cummins (1981), Garcia (1983), and Hernandez-Chavez (1984) have suggested that program "types" for language minority students can be best characterized by their treatment of the native language and English programs:

1. **Additive** programs utilize the student's native language and enhance the student's ability to utilize that language along with English.
2. **Subtractive** programs may or may not use the student's language and serve to enhance English without regard for native language development.

Several forms of subtractive programs are distinguishable:

1. In **submersion** programs students whose proficiency in English is limited are placed in regular classrooms in which English is the language of instruction. They are given no special help in English, nor is their native language used in the classroom.

---

*See Fishman and Lovas (1970), Pacheco (1973), Ramirez (1985), and Ovando and Collier (1985) for more detailed typologies of such programs.

39

2. **English-as-a-Second-Language** programs acknowledge the linguistic ability differences between the student's native language and English, and incorporate English instructional activities to enhance school language learning. The remainder of the schooling is characterized by attributes of the submersion model.

3. **U.S. immersion (or sheltered English)** programs use English, but instructional staff utilize the student's native/home language on a limited basis so as to enhance communication in the classroom. Since knowledge of English is not assumed, the curriculum is modified in vocabulary and pacing, so that program content will be understood.

4. **Transitional bilingual education** programs use the native language as a bridge to the total submersion of the student in English. A concern for native language linguistic and academic content area learning may or may not be encompassed in these programs; however, English learning and English achievement are clearly articulated objectives.

Additive programs also can be distinguished by their emphasis on the native language and English:

1. **Canadian immersion programs** place initial, early grade emphasis on French for native English speakers. Students enter kindergarten or first-grade classes that are conducted by monolingual French-speaking teachers. This early immersion into French is kept rather exclusive of the English until the second or third grade, when English language instruction in the form of a language arts program is introduced for one period per day. By sixth grade, however, both languages share near instructional parity.

2. **Bilingual maintenance** programs target students from two distinct language groups. Their purpose is to achieve proficient bilingualism, both linguistically and academically, in these students. Therefore, instruction is consistently provided in both languages. For those students whose native language is not English, special curricular attention is paid to developing the native language while acquiring English. For those students whose native language is English, particular curricular attention is paid to developing the "target" second language (the native language of student peers).

Conceptually, then, the above distinction between **additive** and **subtractive** education models which serve language minority students is based on the treatment of the native language within the schooling experience of the students. Additive models serve to place significant importance on the native language and English. Subtractive models either place no, some or even extensive emphasis on the utilization of the native language for purposes of enhancing English linguistic and academic competence. Of course, programs can shift their emphasis over time. That is, language minority students may begin in an early grade additive program, which after two to six years is followed by a subtractive program. Moreover, particular instructional practices which are subtractive in nature may be utilized by additive program staff and vice versa. (A good example is the utilization of structured second-language teaching, a common practice of a second-language program, within a bilingual maintenance program.) Therefore, heterogeneity of program efforts in language minority education is the norm.

Programmatic diversity is most likely a function of the children themselves (their linguistic abilities and proportionate concentration), interpretation of federal, state, and local policy, school district staffing, availability of resources, and the specific prevailing community attitudes toward these programs. In the United States, it seems appropriate to conclude, in consideration of such determining factors, that additive programs are rare while several forms of subtractive programs are popular. (Within the public school sector, we are unaware of any K-12 bilingual program whose objective is equal linguistic and academic proficiency in two languages at the time of graduation.)

PROGRAM ATTRIBUTES

Program Assumptions

Empirical and theoretical research contributions related to language minority education and specific educational initiatives have generated several sets of general assumptions which have guided program development and implementation. The California State Department of Education (1984) identifies the following guidelines:

1. Under optimal schooling conditions, on the average, students realize the full academic benefits of their bilingualism only after four to seven years of appropriate instructional treatment.

2. Bilingually schooled students, at times, even under the very best conditions, may initially lag behind their monolingually schooled counterparts in some literacy-based skills. After three or four years, they begin to catch up; and by six or seven years, they equal and commonly surpass their monolingually schooled counterparts.

3. When the instructional treatment is adequately designed and appropriately matched to local sociolinguistic realities, native speakers of a majority language may be schooled in a second language for an average of approximately 50 to 75 percent of the time from kindergarten through the twelfth grade, with no detrimental effects on their academic achievement and native language development. Conversely, it may also be predicted that many language minority students in the United States could be schooled in their native language for an average of 50 to 75 percent of the time from kindergarten through the twelfth grade as an appropriate means to promote their normal academic achievement, high levels of English language proficiency, adequate psychosocial adjustment, and satisfactory native language development.

4. In formal schooling contexts, additive forms of bilingualism are best achieved through the separate use of two languages. That is, as students are instructed in both their first and second languages, steps are taken so that students are exposed to each language at different times and for distinct purposes.

5. To avoid cognitive confusion and greatly increase learning efficiency, program staff should provide initial literacy instruction in bilingual settings in a sequential manner. That is, basic literacy skills should be developed through one language before reading instruction is introduced in the other language.

6. Underachievers and students with learning disabilities seem to experience no detrimental effects from bilingual instruction. When such children receive bilingual schooling, their academic achievement and native language development are similar to those of their counterparts in monolingual programs.

7. Formal second-language instruction, even when provided under optimal conditions, appears to be insufficient to develop all of the language skills needed by second language acquired. Some amount of exposure through natural social interaction is also required. (Calif. State Dept. of Education, 1984, p. 4.)

Wong-Fillmore and Valadez (1985) generate their own similar but expanded set of assumptions which they suggest presently guides much of language minority education in the U.S.:

1. Students who are less than fully proficient in the school language will have difficulty deriving academic benefit from their educational experience, since the inability to understand the language in which instruction is given precludes comprehension of the content of that instruction.

2. It takes LEP students time to acquire the level of proficiency in English that is needed to participate effectively in all-English classes. During the time it takes to learn English, they will get little

out of their school experience if they are instructed exclusively in that language.

3. Instruction in the native language of LEP students allows them to participate in school, and to acquire the skills and knowledge covered in the curriculum while they are learning English. It also allows them to make use of skills, knowledge and experiences they already have, and to build on those prior assets in school.

4. Knowledge and skills are more easily acquired by LEP students in their native language; but computational skills and many literacy skills acquired in the native language can be transferred to the new language once it is mastered. Hence time spent in learning materials in the native language is not time that is lost with respect to the coverage of subject matter in school.

5. Students need adequate exposure to the language of school in order to acquire it as a second language; this exposure to English is best when it takes place in settings in which the learners' special linguistic needs help to shape the way the language gets used. Subject matter instruction which is given in English can provide the exposure that LEP students need, as long as it is appropriately tailored for them. Subject matter instruction in the school language is an essential component of bilingual education.

6. Formal instruction in English as a second language (ESL) can help students get started learning the language. ESL, whether formal or informal, is an integral part of American bilingual education programs.

7. The academic potential of all children, including those served by bilingual programs, have the best chance of being realized when their language skills, their social and cultural experiences, and their knowledge of the world are affirmed in school; these are the foundations of academic development. (Wong-Fillmore and Valadez, 1985.)

These extensive "guides" for language minority program development emphasize several common features related to prominent home/native language use and development. Conversely, "guides" emphasizing minimal or no utilization of the native/home language are also available:

1. This child should receive as much exposure to English as possible in the early years, since this is the fastest way in which the child will learn English.

2. The child will not fall far behind in subject matter learning because children learn many things without understanding the medium of instruction.

3. Learning English is the key to successful school achievement. (Ruiz, 1985, p. 100.)

As is apparent, the educational debate regarding the identification of the "best" programs for language minority students has not been totally resolved. Moreover, having identified "guides" from which the "ideal" may develop does not automatically insure implementation at the program level. How, then, might present educational programs for language minority students be characterized?

Educational Program Features

Survey work by Halcon (1981) and Development Associates (1984) describes some general patterns of language minority instruction in the U.S. Tikenoff (1983) has reported on specific features of effective language minority education. And, a more intensive study by Wong-Fillmore et al. (1985) provides a more detailed analysis of specific educational program variables and their effects on language minority student education. These studies will be highlighted in the following discussion.

Halcon (1981) sampled some 224 schools throughout the United States which had received 3-5 years of federal support for the education of language minority students (Basic Grants, Title VII, ESEA). The findings of that study were summarized into four categories: (a) grade levels served; (b) enrollment characteristics; (c) staff experience; and (d) linguistic characteristics. The following summary of these characteristics describes the structure of a "typical" program at the school site level.

Grade Levels Served. The typical program served either the kindergarten through sixth grade level, or the kindergarten through third grade level. The program did not continue into the junior high or high school. Programs at the upper levels were designed primarily for students entering at this level and who were new to the district. Less than 20 percent of the students eligible for federal program support were identified as participants in the existent federal programs.

Enrollment Characteristics. The typical program had grown in the last five years, both in numbers of classrooms and clients served by them. The average size of the classroom had also increased. Somewhat typically, the school district which sponsored the program was declining in enrollment and was located in an urban area and, in many cases, in a district that was closing schools.

Staffing. On the average, the director of the program had over seven years total experience in education but only five years experience with the specific language minority program in his/her district. On the average, the teachers in these programs had over five years experience (but less than 7) in education but only two to five years experience in the language minority classroom in their respective district. Instructional aides were omnipresent in these programs and had two to five years experience. All of their experience had been in the language minority program (usually in his/her respective district).

Language-Use Characteristics. Sampled programs reported English was the language most widely used in bilingual programs. In addition, no program indicated the non-use or limited use of English in the classroom. However, limited or non-use of the native/home language was reported.

In summary, the "typical" program, as described in this profile, does not place emphasis on native language instruction. The data reveals that English was the language used by the majority of programs. Moreover, few children were given the opportunity to continue with their bilingual instruction after elementary school. Programs at the upper grade levels were intended primarily for students entering and not for those continuing. Staff which implemented programs was relatively inexperienced in the education of language minority students. Most administrators (program directors, coordinators, federal program officers, etc.) had less than seven years experience in education. Relatively few (22%) teachers had over three years educational experience in general. Half as many had three years experience in language minority program classrooms. Finally, instructional aides were utilized extensively for instructional purposes (Halcon, 1981).

In contrast to Halcon's study of only federal programs serving language minority students, Development Associates (1984) conducted a study of such programs regardless of funding source. They sampled grades K-5 in 335 schools, in 191 public school districts, representing 19 states. The number of schools selected in each state was determined by using a probability sampling formula taking into account the proportion of language minority students in the state. Use of this sampling technique allowed the study to make broader generalizations (weighted estimates) regarding the character of instruction for language minority students in the U.S. This study utilized local school district definitions of language minority students and data reported by these school districts.

Students Served. In estimating the number of language minority students served, the authors of the study recommended caution regarding their estimates. The estimates were considered conservative because:

1. The sampling of the kindergarten and grade 6 LM-LEP (language minority-limited English proficient) populations was statistically restricted;

2. Pressures existed in some districts and schools to understate their LM-LEP counts in order to show high percentages of such students being served; and

3. Some teachers reported being aware of students not labelled as LM-LEP who needed LM-LEP services. (Development Associates, 1984, p. 3-25.)

The findings of this study suggest that in 1983-84, based on local definitions and information supplied by local district officials (Development Associates, 1984):

1. A reported 94 percent of the identified language minority students were receiving some form of special services.

2. Approximately 76 percent of these students had Spanish as the native language.

3. Sampled schools reported three to four times as many Grade 1 students as Grade 5 students.

4. Some 20 percent of these students were mainstreamed into all-English medium classrooms during the year.

5. Schools with smaller enrollments of these students mainstreamed a greater percentage.

6. In the 10 states which account for over 80 percent of the U.S. language minority student population, some 25 percent of schools reported that 11-20 percent of their student body were LM-LEP; 27 percent of these schools reported their population of LM-LEP students was 21 percent or more. These estimates suggest that in these 10 states, over 50 percent of schools in each state have 10 percent or more language minority student enrollments.

In general, this study reports an extremely high (94%) special service provision index for language minority student populations. The exact nature of the special treatment remains unclear. However, it is significant that districts report such a high incidence of "special" treatment for language minority students. Halcon (1981) reported less than 20 percent of eligible language minority students were receiving treatment provided by federal funds. The Development Associates (1984) data suggest that resources other than those from the federal government were being utilized for special language minority student instruction. The data (Development Associates, 1984) support other findings (Halcon, 1981; O'Malley, 1982) regarding: (a) the higher proportion of language minority students in the early grades; (b) concentration of students in specific states; and (c) a large number of students which move yearly from "special" programs to "mainstreamed" programs.

Staffing. The staffing of language minority programs reported by Development Associates is highly similar to that reported by Halcon (1981):

1. The schools serving language minority students in grades 1-5 had 4.0 teachers, 3.5 paraprofessionals and 1.1 resource or instructional support staff (paraprofessional and/or professional).

2. Teachers of language minority students had a medium 10.7 years of teaching experience in grades K-6, and 5.8 years of experience teaching language minority students; however, over 50 percent of these teachers had 3 or less years experience in teaching language minority students.

3. Only 50 percent of the teachers primarily responsible for language minority student instruction reported speaking a language other than English, and only 28 percent of these teachers had obtained language minority education related credentials.

This staffing information continues to suggest that paraprofessionals are utilized extensively in instructional programs for language minority students. In addition, professional teachers for these students are less experienced and not likely to have received specific credential-related professional training, with more than 50 percent unable to speak the language of the student.

Language-Use Characteristics. For those schools sampled by Developmental Associates (1984), several salient features were reported:

1. Eight separate "treatments" regarding the use of the native language were identified, ranging from only the use of native language to total non-use of the native language.

2. Ninety-three percent of the schools sampled reported that use of English was a key ingredient (received emphasis) in their programs; 7 percent, conversely, indicated that use of the native language was the key ingredient.

3. Sixty percent of the sampled schools reported that both the native/home language and English were utilized during instruction.

4. Thirty percent of the sampled schools reported minimal use of the native language; only 3 percent reported use of English only.

A majority of these schools (60%) utilized the native language to some degree, while a minority of these schools (30%) utilized it to a lesser degree. However, a clear majority of these schools (93%) reported that English dominated the instructional programs.

The above studies indicate that a variety of programs for language minority students presently exists. However, this population of students seems to be extensively underserved by federal programs, is likely to receive instruction from less experienced and paraprofessional staff, is served in the primary grades, and is in classrooms where English clearly predominates but not without some use of the student's native language.

"Effective" Instructional Variables

Tikenoff (1983) in the report of the Significant Bilingual Instructional Features Study (SBIF) reports commonalities in the organization and instruction of effective language minority classrooms. The 58 classrooms observed in this study come from six sites and include a variety of non-English languages. All were considered "effective" on two criteria: first, they were nominated by members of four constituencies — teachers, other school personnel, students and parents; second, the teaching behaviors produced rates of "academic learning time" (ALT) — a measure of student engagement on academic tasks — as high or higher than reported in other effective teaching research.

The SBIF findings can be divided into two parts: (1) instructional features common to bilingual and monolingual education and (2) instructional features unique to bilingual education.

Shared Instructional Features. An initial set of instructional features identified in the 58 effective classrooms pertain to the delivery and organization of instruction:

1. Successful teachers of LEP (limited English proficient) students specify task outcomes and what students must do to accomplish tasks competently. In addition, they communicate (a) high expectations for LEP students in terms of learning, and (b) a sense of efficacy in terms of their own ability to teach.

2. Successful teachers of LEP students, like effective teachers generally, exhibit use of "active teaching" behaviors which have been found to be related to increased student performance on academic tests of achievement in reading and mathematics, including: (a) communicating clearly when giving directions, specifying tasks, and presenting new information; (b) obtaining and maintaining students' engagement in instructional tasks by pacing instruction appropriately, promoting involvement, and communicating their expectations for students' success in completing instructional tasks; (c) monitoring students' progress; and (d) providing im-

mediate feedback whenever required regarding the students' success.

Unique Instructional Features. Instructional features unique to language minority student education included the use of two languages, special activities for teaching a second language, and instructional practices that took advantage of students' cultural background.

According to SBIF reports, averaged across the 58 classrooms in the SBIF study, English was used approximately 60 percent of the time, and L1 or a combination of the two was used the rest of the time, with the percentage of English increasing with grade level. An additional significant instructional feature was the particular way in which the two languages were often combined:

1. Successful teachers for LEP students mediated instruction for LEP students by the use of the students' native language and English for instruction, alternating between the two languages whenever necessary to ensure clarity of instruction. Although this type of language switching occurred, teachers did not translate directly from one language to another.

2. Students learned the language of instruction when engaged in instructional tasks using that language. This integrative approach to developing English language skills during ongoing instruction in the regular classroom contrasts with the more traditional pullout procedures where LEP students leave the regular instructional setting to receive ESL instruction.

The SBIF study reports that the use of information from the LEP students' home culture can promote engagement in instructional tasks and contribute to a feeling of trust between children and their teachers. The SBIF researchers found three ways in which home and community culture is incorporated into classroom life: Cultural referents in both verbal and non-verbal forms are used to communicate instructional and institutional demands; instruction is organized to build upon rules of discourse from the L1 culture; and values and norms of the L1 culture are respected equally with those of the school. The SBIF report provides a particular example from a Navajo classroom:

> One entire group of LEP students was observed as "loud, pushy and aggressive" with their Anglo teacher, behavior which was never observed while they were with their Navajo teacher.... The Navajo teacher, whether teaching through English or Navajo, seemed to have established with the class a set of Navajo-based ground rules. These in-

cluded creating a non-competitive atmosphere and avoiding bringing attention in any way to individual children. The teacher accomplished this by not calling students by name, accepting answers which were called out and by not insisting on children raising their hands. The other teacher who instructed in English exclusively seemed to operate with Anglo-based ground rules which were in direct opposition to those established by the Navajo teacher. (Goodman, 1984, p. 13.)

The cultural appropriateness of teaching practices is identified as important as the language of instruction in achieving students' maximum attention to the task at hand.

Effective Oral Language Development. Wong-Fillmore et al. (1985) provide a detailed analysis regarding the influence of classroom practices on the development of oral English in Hispanic and Chinese background language minority students. In this study, 17 Hispanic and Chinese language minority student classrooms (13 third grades and 4 fifth grades) served as sites. These students were in classrooms which either utilized both the native language and English during instruction or utilized only English instruction. Specific measures of oral English language production and comprehension were obtained over a one-year period. In addition, classroom observations documented the character of teacher-student interaction, student-student interaction, as well as the organizational features of instruction. A companion study directly evaluated the effect of classroom practices on those students who had minimal (0-1 years) exposure to English.

These authors report a series of potentially significant observations:

1. Instructional practices which promoted oral English language development were related to the students' initial level of oral English proficiency. Less proficient speakers of English benefitted more from high levels of teacher and peer interaction.

2. The instructional variables related to enhanced English development were different for Hispanic and Chinese background students. Chinese students seemed to do best in classrooms in which the instructional style was characterized by teacher-directed instruction. Hispanic students demonstrated enhanced English oral language development under classroom conditions in which more opportunities to interact with English-speaking peers existed.

The Hispanic students were much more sensitive to the quality of instruction they received than were the Chinese, who, from all evidence, tended to compensate for teacher differences. The conditions that favored the Chinese children (teacher-directed learning in quiet, tightly controlled, work-oriented environments) matched the conditions most comfortable for American teachers, whereas the conditions that favored Hispanic children (group-centered, cooperative learning in somewhat more open, socially oriented classroom environments) are more difficult for teachers.

In addition, these researchers reported that development of English production and comprehension was related to several attributes of student-teacher interaction. Teachers who adjusted their linguistic interaction based on student feedback were more likely to produce English language gains. Such adjustments included simplification of syntax, less rapid speech, and repetition. Allowing and encouraging student participation and calling attention to the structure of language while using it were additional enhancing characteristics.

This report, much like the SBIF study, suggests strongly that teachers can play a significant role in English language development for language minority students. Moreover, this study like others (Garcia, Flores and Carrasco, 1982; Krashen, 1984) identifies the potential importance of peer interaction for English language acquisition and the influence of initial English language proficiency levels on English acquisition. However, this study indicates the importance of ethnolinguistic student differences (specifically those between Hispanic and Chinese language minority students).

Literacy is an academic "skill" or "ability" which is directly related to language. Wong-Fillmore and Valadez (1985) summarize empirical research in the domain of literacy instruction. They conclude:

1. LEP students can acquire decoding skills relatively easily, even when they do not speak English. However, they have considerably greater difficulty making sense of the materials they read (Cziko, 1978).
2. Initial reading instruction in L1 has the effect of later success in L2 reading. The ability to read in L1 once acquired transfers to L2 (Medrano, 1973; Rosier, 1977).
3. Efforts to develop L2 literacy without oral language training in L2 are unlikely to succeed. Students taught literacy skills in L1 may take longer to learn L2 literacy, but they make greater gains over time (Engle, 1975).

Similarly, Goodman, Goodman and Flores (1979), after a review of their own work with Papago and Spanish native language students, concluded:

In our experience we've found that if bilingual speakers are literate in another language, their development of literacy in English will be easier than for people not literate in any language; and further, their control of English will be speeded as a result of their rapid progress in becoming literate in English. All this assumes that oral and written English are equally needed and functional and that the opportunity to use both are present. (Goodman et al., 1979, p. 22.)

It is presently difficult to identify all the significant variables that promote "effective" instruction for language minority students. More data is becoming available, particularly in the area of language and literacy development (Thonis, 1981; Wong-Fillmore et al., 1985, Garcia and Flores, 1986). This is not to suggest that "effective" programs for language minority students are nonexistent. The discussion above highlights research which has identified such program attributes.

PROGRAM EVALUATION

Programs designed for language minority students have been evaluated to determine their effectiveness in comparison with programs designed for native English-speaking students. Evaluators admit that the number of variables influencing these evaluations make sound evaluations difficult. Such variables include the diversity of federal, state and local policy (and specific implementation of these policies), the linguistic and ethnic populations served, curriculum content, teaching strategies, program resources, quantity and quality of staffing, and degree of school/community support. As the following discussion demonstrates, however, such a conclusion does not suggest that such evaluative research is unavailable.

The Canadian Experience

Lambert and Tucker (1972) provide one of the few extensive evaluations of the bilingual education effort. The St. Lambert experiment involved the immersion of native English-speaking children in an elementary French schooling experience. Although the formal educational program did not incorporate English as an area of curricular importance until the second or third grade, these children continued to live in home environments almost totally dominated by English speakers. The evaluation of the program was longitudinal in nature and obtained several measures of the children's academic, linguistic, and intellectual progress, and compared these measures with those of children participating in all English and French educational programs. Students were equated on several relevant indices: (a) age, (b) general intelligence, (c) socioeconomic status, and (d) family motivation for academic success.

The effects of the program were overwhelmingly positive. First, very few substantive differences between experimental (bilingual) and control (English and French) groups were reported on the multitude of measures obtained. Some differences were observed during the first one or two years, especially differences between bilingual and monolingual French groups. Monolingual French speakers outperformed their bilingual counterparts on French linguistic and academic measures. But by the fifth year, no substantive differences on intellectual, academic or linguistic measures were apparent across groups. A later report by Barik, Lambert and Tucker (1974) on these same groups, after seven years, finds the same pattern of results.

It seems difficult to argue with these extremely impressive results. Children who began schooling in a language foreign to their own homes were able to acquire and achieve the same educational objectives in two languages without detrimental effects and within the same temporal period as those children participating in "traditional" monolingual programs. Similar effects of programs in Canada have been informally and formally (Barik and Swain, 1975) reported. Thus, this immersion model has been adopted extensively throughout the French/English-speaking provinces of Canada.

Program Effectiveness in the U.S.

Although many evaluations have been made of the effectiveness of bilingual education programs, a great deal of controversy still exists regarding the best method for educating language minority children. Two studies have been used repeatedly by policymakers to argue that language minority students do better or at least as well without instruction in their native language: a study conducted by the American Institutes for Research in 1974 with a contract from the then U.S. Office of Education (Danoff et al., 1977a & b, 1978), and an extensive review of the literature on the effectiveness of bilingual education conducted by the U.S. Department of Education's Office of Planning, Budget, and Evaluation (Baker and de Kanter, 1981, 1982).

Danoff and colleagues examined students in grades 2-6 in all Title VII Spanish/English bilingual projects in their fourth or fifth year of funding and comparable students not enrolled in such programs. They found that less than one-third of the students were in bilingual programs because of their need for English instruction (as judged by the classroom teacher) and that across grades, in general, Title VII students were performing worse in English and at the same level in math as students in the comparison group.

After reviewing 300 primary evaluations, 28 of which were methodologically sound enough to include in a review, Baker and de Kanter concluded that "transitional bilingual education (TBE) should not be the sole approach for instructing language-minority students since there is no firm evidence that TBE is uniquely effective in raising language-minority students' performance in English and in non-language subject areas" (as compared with submersion, English as a second language (ESL), or immersion).

These two studies, as well as other evaluations of bilingual education programs, have been criticized by numerous researchers (Cardenas, 1977; Gray, 1977; Zappert and Cruz, 1977; O'Malley, 1978; Troike, 1978; Hernandez-Chavez et al., 1982; Yates and Ortiz, 1983; McLaughlin, 1985). A recent critique by Willig (1985) sums up much of the criticism. In many studies, treatment and control groups are not comparable because random assignments are ineffective or create even more problems, which Willig discusses in detail. For example, equating students on absolute proficiency in both languages is problematic for both statistical and assessment reasons. One statistical problem is regression toward the mean, which can create the impression that students in bilingual programs do worse on posttests than on pretests while comparison students do better. Willig also notes that models of reliability-corrected covariance analysis are not effective unless the instruments used are reliable; language tests that are used to determine entry and exit into bilingual programs have low reliability and low convergent validity. Other factors that contribute to non-comparable groups include: differential amounts of English language exposure both in the school and neighborhood setting; comparison groups that are made up of students who are more English proficient than the treatment groups and either do not qualify for the bilingual program or had already graduated from the program; changes in the group composition between the pretest and posttest, with more qualified students moving out of the bilingual program (in some instances, into the comparison group) and less proficient students moving into the experimental group; the instability of bilingual programs, exemplified by high rates of teacher turnover; and by the disorganization and hostile or uninterested attitudes of non-bilingual staff in the schools. Another serious problem mentioned by

Hakuta and Snow (1986) is that the enormous amount of diversity within programs labeled "bilingual" and programs labeled "other" (e.g. submersion, immersion, English as a second language) makes comparisons between program types extraordinarily difficult.

One of the best efforts to date to evaluate the overall effectiveness of bilingual education was conducted by Willig (1985). Unlike Baker and de Kanter who used a narrative approach, she used meta-analysis (Glass, 1978; Glass, McGaw and Smith, 1981), a more powerful statistical procedure, and did all the coding from an original version of the studies rather than from summaries and second-person reviews. From her analysis, she concluded that a positive effect is produced by (a) bilingual program participation when compared with submersion, and (b) bilingual program participation including English as a second language when compared with submersion including English as a second language, when other important sources of variation are held constant.

Summary. What seems clear-cut regarding the evaluation of language minority education programs is that future evaluation and analysis of these programs must be more useful. State and federal policymakers are interested in knowing whether funds invested in language minority education make a favorable difference in educational outcomes. Would the children do worse in school if these targeted funds did not exist? Some policymakers are also interested in which program model works best and for which students. For example, a current federally funded study (Ramirez, 1986) examines academic outcome difference for language minority students placed in these different programs (English, immersion, early exit bilingual, and late exit bilingual). For educators interested in the overall improvement of language minority education, different evaluations are necessary. Future useful evaluations must identify the specific attributes of successful programs. These evaluations must take into consideration the individual differences among children including their language and culture, as well as school-related variables such as curriculum, personnel, and community support.

SUMMARY AND CONCLUSION

Classroom instructional activity for language minority students differs depending on answers to the following interrelated questions:

1. What are the L1 and L2 characteristics of the students, families and communities?

2. What model of instruction is desired?
   a. How do we choose to utilize L1 and L2 **as mediums of instruction**?
   b. How do we choose to handle the **instruction** of L1 and L2?
3. What is the nature of staff and resources necessary to implement the desired instruction?

Language minority education programs are as diverse as there are the permutations of potential answers to these questions. Yet, in all this diversity, "effective" programs for language minority students are presently available. The "state of the art" of such programs has significantly changed since initial U.S. policy activity in 1967, and, no doubt, educational programming for language minority students will continue to receive research, practice and policy attention, and will evolve as a result of that attention.

Chapter 4

LITIGATION POLICY

FOUNDATIONS OF LANGUAGE MINORITY
STUDENT "RIGHTS"

IN MOST educational matters, courts have attempted to define and apply basic principles but refrain from prescribing or formulating educational policy. The simple message of *Brown v. Board of Education* (1954), precluding segregation of public school students by race, was easily adaptable to other identifiable student populations, such as handicapped, limited English proficient, or female students. The applicable principle was accessible and compelling: equal treatment before the institutions of society.

Plaintiffs pursued other issues beyond gaining access: Equal treatment and equal outcomes. Once admitted to the system "equally," they wanted the schools to provide resources to meet special needs enabling them to compete equally with more advantaged peers. Furthermore, schools were asked to insure that educational outcomes be equivalent. The principle of equal opportunity and/or treatment had to be adapted to these complex aspirations and became a demand for educational programs and practices which would accomplish the appropriate outcomes.

The courts were confronted with a distasteful task. The level of plaintiff demand was clear: status quo is inappropriate ("the educational treatment is wrong"), and fix it ("this type of program will do it"). Courts were asked to designate specific curricula or methodologies, as well as minimally satisfactory educational results. Courts had traditionally avoided educational policy disputes and had refused to select among pedagogic or curricular choices (Rist and Anson, 1977). That reluctance must have seemed all the more warranted as plaintiffs and defendants produced a procession of experts, emphatically describing alternatives, irreconcilable theoretical realities, and discounting opposing view-points. Hence, conclusive answers to rather basic questions remained quite elusive (e.g. Does integration positively affect academic achieve-ment? Do increased expenditures on education influence student achievement?).

Consequently, courts became educational reformers but did so reluc-tantly and cautiously, attempting to avoid involvement in professional debates regarding pedagogy. Judges began to attend meticulously to the proper demarcation between principle and policy, determined to take action only when the occasional flagrant exclusion or discrimination case arose. However, through several decades of adjudication, policy de-rived from that adjudication has arisen. The following discussion high-lights five distinct federal cases which have defined that judicial policy specific to language minority education: *Lau v. Nichols*, 1974; *Aspira of New York v. New York Board of Education*, 1975; *U.S. v. Texas*, 1981; *Cas-teñeda v. Pickard*, 1981; and *Keyes v. Denver Public School District #1*, 1983. These cases along with corollary decisions will be discussed in detail. However, these cases rested on the following legislative and administra-tive foundations:

1. **The 1964 Civil Rights Act.** Legislatively, Title VI of the 1964 Civil Rights Act banned discrimination on the grounds of race, color, or national origin in any program receiving federal financial assistance. A federal regulation following from this act banned re-cipients of federal funds from "restricting an individual in any way in the enjoyment of any advantage or privilege enjoyed by others receiving any service, financial aid or benefit under the (federally funded) program. An accompanying provision of this regulation indicated that a recipient of federal funds may not utilize criteria or methods which have the effect of impairing accomplishment of the objectives of the federally funded program with respect to indi-viduals of a particular race, color, or national origin. Significantly, under this act, failure of an institution to comply with pursuant regulations provided the possibility of a private cause of action (a lawsuit) to rectify the situation. Therefore, students need not wait for the government to enforce the law, instead they may be able to sue so that an appropriate program is implemented. Because al-most all public schools receive federal money and the mandate was dependent on the recipient of **any** federal funding, the mandate af-fected almost all schools.

2. **The May 25, 1970 Memorandum**. The Department of Health, Education and Welfare memorandum provided the following clarification of previous regulations related to the 1964 Civil Rights Act: "Where inability to speak and understand the English language excludes national origin minority group children from effective participation in the educational program offered by a school district, the district must take affirmative steps to rectify the language deficiency in order to open instructional programs to these students." This was the first "quasi-legal" mandate which required provision of special services to language minority students.

3. **The 1974 Equal Educational Opportunities and Transportation of Students Act (and related regulations)**. This act makes "the failure by an educational agency to take appropriate action to overcome language barriers that impede equal participation by its students in its instructional programs" an unlawful denial of equal educational opportunity. This act suggests that any child, irrespective of language, is entitled to language assistance programs if the student can show that participation in school is impeded by a language-related attribute.

These laws, regulations and related policy have served to guide the actions of the courts. The U.S. Constitution has also been used to coax the court's intervention on behalf of language minority students. However, resultant litigation policies have returned consistently to the above foundations.

CASE LAW

Lau v. Nichols (1974). There is a clear starting point for the development of court-related policy regarding language minority students: the 1974 United States Supreme Court decision in *Lau v. Nichols*. This case originated in San Francisco and involved a claim by a class of non-English-speaking Chinese students that they were being denied equal educational opportunity. The court suit was filed on March 25, 1970 and involved 12 American-born and foreign-born Chinese students. Parents of these students requested that the San Francisco School district meet the recognized needs of non-English-speaking Chinese students in its schools. Prior to the suit, in 1966, at the request of parents, an ESL pullout program was initiated by the district, and in a 1967 school census, the district identified 2,456 limited-English-speaking

Chinese students. By 1970, the district had identified 2,856 such students. Of this number more than half (1,790) received no special instruction. In addition, over 2,600 of these students were taught by teachers who could not themselves speak Chinese. It is important to note that:

1. The district was not unaware of the number of students in need of special language services; and
2. The district had made initial, although admittedly meager, attempts to serve this population.

Therefore, the district was formally conscious of the problem and attempted to address it. On May 26, 1970 the federal district court found that the district had no legal obligation to provide the special services but encouraged the district as an educational policy to attempt to address the problem as an educational (as opposed to legal) obligation to these students. On January 8, 1973, the Ninth Circuit District Court of Appeals upheld this lower court ruling. Plaintiffs appealed to the U.S. Supreme Court.

The Supreme Court's majority opinion overruled the appeals court in favor of the pupils and parents. The opinion relied on statutory (legislative) grounds in granting relief, and avoided any reference to constitutional determination, although plaintiffs had argued that the equal protection clause (Fourteenth Amendment) of the U.S. Constitution was relevant to the case. Pupils' right to special education services flowed from the district's obligations under Title VI of the 1964 Civil Rights Act and the Health Education and Welfare qualifying regulation articulated in its May 25, 1970 memorandum. The plaintiffs did not request an explicit remedy, such as a bilingual or ESL program, nor did the court address this issue. Thus, *Lau v. Nichols* does not stand for the proposition that children must receive a particular educational service (such as bilingual, bicultural instruction or ESL) but instead that some form of effective educational programming must be available to "open the instruction" to language minority students.

Thus, *Lau v. Nichols* was a distinct starting point for taking into consideration language minority student status. It was based on Title VI of the 1964 Civil Rights Act. Further, the opinion quoted HEW guidelines (the May 25 memorandum) which were quite firm in requiring extra services from the districts to assist language minority students.

Although cases were litigated to ensure compliance with the *Lau* requirement for some special assistance, subsequent cases more often dealt with issues left unanswered in *Lau v. Nichols*: Who are these students? What form of additional educational services must be provided?

Aspira of New York, Inc., v. Board of Education (1975). As Roos (1978) indicates, the issue of who "requires" special language assistance has not been clearly delineated by the courts. In *Aspira of New York, Inc. v. Board of Education* (1975), a suit was brought by a community action group on behalf of all Hispanic children in the New York School District whose English language deficiency prevented effective participation in an English schooling context and who could effectively participate in a Spanish language curriculum (Roos, 1978). The district court hearing this case adopted a language dominance procedure to identify those students eligible for non-English, Spanish language instructional programs. The procedure called for parallel examinations to obtain language proficiency estimates on Spanish and English standardized achievement tests. All students scoring below the twentieth percentile on this test were given the same (or parallel) achievement test in Spanish. If the student scored higher on the Spanish achievement test and Spanish language proficiency test, the student was to be placed in a Spanish language program, defined in practice as a transitional bilingual education program. These procedures assumed adequate reliability and validity for those language and achievement tests administered. Such an assumption was and still is highly questionable. However, the court argued that it acted in a "reasonable manner," admitting that in the absence of better assessment procedures it was forced to follow previous *(Lau v. Nichols)* precedents.

A subsequent case, *Otero v. Mesa County School District No. 51*, (1977) concluded that a clear relationship between low academic achievement and the English language deficiency of students must be clearly demonstrated before a court could mandate special language services for language minority students. This court suggested that in the absence of this clear relationship, low academic achievement could be attributed to other variables (e.g. low socioeconomic background). Therefore, merely showing that Spanish is the home language was insufficient to require a school district to provide special language assistance. Instead, a linkage between non-English proficiency and low school achievement must be established. Therefore, the legal obligation related to providing a special educational program for language minority students has become based on the link between lack of English proficiency and the lack of English school achievement.

Castañeda v. Pickard (1981). In Arizona, a suit was filed against a local school district by a non-profit corporation, suing on behalf of the children of a community of 5,000 persons, most of whom were of Mexican/American or Yaqui ancestry *(Guadalupe v. Tempe School District No. 3*; 1976). Plaintiffs organized their lawsuit around the claim that the district was acting discriminatorily in failing to provide these children with appropriate educational programs. This district curriculum failed to recognize the special educational needs of students from Mexican/American or Yaqui descent. The curriculum did not reflect the historical contributions of people of appellants' descent to the state of Arizona and the United States. Plaintiffs requested a maintenance bilingual program, which would ensure competence at graduation in the child's native language and English, with biculturalism reflected throughout the curriculum.

The district court entered judgment for the school district, and the plaintiffs appealed to the Ninth Circuit, which put the dispute to rest by affirming the lower court's order. In their opinion, it is noted that plaintiffs never claimed that the district was not attempting to serve the special needs of language minority students. The court concluded, in its constitutional holding, "we hold, therefore, that the Constitution neither requires nor prohibits the bilingual and bicultural education sought by appellants. Such matters are for the people to decide." In assessing the choices made by Congress in Civil Rights Act of 1964 and the Equal Educational Opportunity Act of 1974, the court concluded that in previous litigation, courts also have not required districts to provide what the plaintiffs sought, even as a condition for receipt of federal funds. As long as the district responds appropriately to the needs of LEP children, effectively remediating their English language deficiency, no federal statute has been violated. Essentially, the court failed to find any statutory or constitutional violation committed by the district.

However, in the key fifth circuit court decision of *Castañeda v. Pickard* (1981), the court interpreted Section 1703(f) of the Equal Education Opportunity Act of 1974 as substantiating the holding of *Lau v. Nichols* that schools cannot ignore the special language needs of students. Moreover, this court then pondered whether the statutory requirement that districts take "appropriate action" suggested a more precise obligation than the Civil Rights Act requirement that districts do something. Plaintiffs predictably urged on the court a construction of "appropriate action" necessitating at least Bilingual Transitional Programs. The court concluded, however, that Section 1703(f) did not embody a congressional mandate that any particular form of remedy be uniformly adopted. If Congress wished to intrude so extraordinarily on the local districts' traditional curricular discretion, it must speak more explicitly. This conclusion, the court argued, was buttressed by the congressional use of "appropriate action" in the statute, instead of bilingual education or any other educational terminology.

However, the court concluded that Congress did require districts to adopt an appropriate program, and by creating a cause of action in federal court to enforce Section 1703(f), it left to federal judges the task of determining whether a given program is appropriate. The court noted that Congress had not provided guidance in the statute and its brief legislative history on what it intended by selecting "appropriateness" as the operative standard. Continuing with clear reluctance and hesitancy, the court described a mode of analysis for a Section 1703(f) case:

1. The court will determine whether the district's program is "informed by an educational theory recognized as sound by some experts in the field or, at least, deemed a legitimate experimental strategy." The court explicitly declined to be an arbiter among competing theorists. The appropriate question is whether some justification exists, not the relative merits of competing alternatives.
2. The court will determine whether the district is implementing its program in a reasonably effective manner (e.g. adequate funding, qualified staffing).
3. The court will determine whether the program, after operating long enough to be a legitimate trial, produces results indicating language barriers are being overcome. A plan which is initially appropriate may have to be revised if expectations are not met or if the district's circumstances significantly change, so that the original plan is no longer sufficient.

After *Castañeda v. Pickard*, it became legally possible to substantiate a violation of Section 1703(f), following from *Lau v. Nichols*, on three grounds:

1. The program providing special language services to eligible language minority students is not based on sound educational theory;
2. The program is not being implemented in an effective manner; and
3. The program, after a period of "reasonable implementation," does not produce results that substantiates that language barriers are being overcome.

It is obvious from these three that a local school district may continue to be at liberty to implement a program with some educational theoretical support, and the courts will allow it to implement such a program for a "reasonable" time before it will make judgments upon its "positive" or "negative" effects. However, the *Castañeda v. Pickard* court, again reluctantly but firmly, spoke to the issue of program implementation. Particularly, the court indicated that the district must provide adequate resources, including trained instructional personnel, materials and other relevant support which would insure effective program implementation. Therefore, a district which chooses a particular program model for addressing the needs of its language minority students must demonstrate that its staffing and materials are adequate for such a program. Implicit is the requirement that a district staff its program with language minority education specialists, typically defined by state-approved credentials or professional course work (similar devices utilized to judge professional expertise in other areas of professional education).

U.S. v. Texas (1981). This is a parallel case to *Castañeda v. Pickard*. The case was initiated against the Texas Education Agency, a state as opposed to a local educational agency. As first filed on March 6, 1970, the U.S. Department of Justice (plaintiffs in this action) claimed that the state agency had failed to oversee local school districts' actions related to the desegregation of Texas schools. The federal district court in 1971 found the state agency delinquent in its duty, and after subsequent unsuccessful appeals by the state agency, the agency was ordered to develop a state plan for implementing desegregation statewide. A component of that order (Section G) addressed the issue of eliminating the vestiges of discrimination based on language barriers (Leibowitz, 1982). Following this order, the state agency prepared an 86-page report (and plan), in which a 17-page section was included, "Alternative Programs to Improve Curriculum for Minority Students." Therefore, the state agency met the requirements of the mandated order and, in doing so, indicated the need for alternative educational programs which addressed the needs of language minority students in the alternative program section.

Significantly, on July 10, 1972, a motion to intervene, filed by the GI Forum and the League of Latin American Citizens (both community groups with a history of desegregation litigation regarding Hispanics in Texas), allowed these parties to participate in the action as representatives of persons of Mexican-American ancestry. Subsequently, on June 3, 1975, these organizations filed an action seeking enforcement of Section G of the 1971 order, and requested supplemental relief (action by the state agency) for Mexican-American students in Texas schools who were limited in their English proficiency. They requested that the state agency require bilingual instruction and compensatory programs. The United States Department of Justice (the original plaintiff) joined in a similar request for enforcement of Section G.

In the *U.S. v. Texas* (1981) decision, the district court spoke to the responsibility of the state agency and to the type of program which should be implemented particularly in reference to the Equal Educational Opportunity Act of 1974:

1. The state's compensatory education program has not succeeded in eradicating the disabling effects of pervasive historical discrimination suffered by Mexican-Americans in the field of education. Bilingual instruction is uniquely suited to remedying the special learning problems of these children and preparing them to enjoy equal educational opportunity in the Texas public schools. The state's existing bilingual program, while an improvement over past practices, is wholly inadequate.

2. Serious flaws permeate every aspect of the state's effort. Required program content, described in detail by state law and regulation, is frequently ignored by local school districts. The scanty coverage of the state's bilingual program leaves tens of thousands of Mexican-American children without the compensatory help they require to function effectively as students. Identification of limited English proficient students by local school districts is unreliable and unverified. Criteria for transferring students out of bilingual programs and into all-English classrooms are fixed far too low to ensure that all vestiges of discrimination have been removed before relief is cut off. Finally, the state has failed to monitor local bilingual programs in a thorough and diligent manner or to enforce applicable laws and regulations through the imposition of sanctions in appropriate circumstances. Since the defendants have not remedied these serious deficiencies, meaningful relief for the victims of unlawful discrimination must be instituted by court decree.

3. It is true that bilingual instruction per se is not required by Section 1703(f) or any other provision of law. If the defendants here had implemented another type of program which effectively overcame the language barriers of Mexican-American students and enabled them to participate equally in the school curriculum, without using bilingual instruction of any kind, such a course would constitute "appropriate action" and preclude statutory relief. But the evi-

dence in this case, discussed above, showed that the defendants had failed to remedy this serious educational problem as it exists throughout the state of Texas. A violation of Section 1703(f) had thus occurred. The evidence also demonstrated that bilingual instruction is uniquely suited to meet the needs of the state's Spanish-speaking students. Therefore, the defendants would be required to take further steps, including additional bilingual instruction, if needed, to satisfy their affirmative obligation under the statute and enforce the right of these linguistically deprived children to equal educational opportunity.

Almost immediately, the Texas legislature passed sweeping new language minority education legislation which addressed many of the issues identified by the court in *U.S. v. Texas*. On July 13, 1982, the Fifth U.S. Circuit Court of Appeals reversed the decision. It did so on several grounds; however, the most compelling was that the 1981 Texas law, which requires bilingual education in elementary school districts, made the previous case moot. The case was remanded to the district court for reconsideration and with the concern that the state law (and the programs generated by that law) be given a "reasonable" time to display effects (as per the *Castañeda v. Pickard* standard).

Keyes v. School District No. 1, Denver (1983). This action was originally initiated in 1969 by a class of minority parents, on behalf of their minor children attending the Denver Public Schools, to desegregate the public schools and to provide equal education opportunities for all children. In granting the preliminary injunction, the trial court found that during the previous decade the school board had willfully undertaken to maintain and intensify racial segregation, *Keyes v. School District No. 1*, Denver, Colorado (1969). The court ordered boundary changes to desegregate the Denver public schools. Years of litigation ensued with multiple appeals to the court of appeals and the Supreme Court. In 1973, the district court concluded that the Denver Public School system was an unlawful dual system in violation of the United States Constitution and ordered the dismantling of the dual system (*Keyes v. School District No. 1*, Denver, Colorado [1973]).

In 1974, during the development of a desegregation plan, intervention was sought by the Congress of Hispanic Educators (CHE) on behalf of themselves as educators and on behalf of their minor children who attended the Denver schools. CHE was interested in ensuring that the desegregation plan ordered by the court included the educational treatment of language minority students to overcome the deficits created by numerous years of attendance in segregated and inferior schools. A sequence of additional proceedings and negotiations followed with final comprehensive court hearings commencing in May 1982.

In December 1983, Judge Richard Matsch issued a 31-page opinion, which is the most lengthy and complete language programming discussion to date in a judicial decision. Judge Matsch, applying the *Castañeda v. Pickard* standards, found that Denver had failed to direct adequate resources to its language program, with teacher skills a major concern.

Following this decision, a landmark remedial plan was negotiated. As a result of the plan, the Denver Public Schools have: (a) hired a staff of 75 trained ESL teachers; (b) expanded bilingual programs from 11 to 32 schools; (c) set standards for bilingual teachers; (d) revamped the curriculum for limited-English-proficient students, so that it is consistent with the curriculum provided other students; (e) established an accountability program for assessing student progress; and (f) established special programs for Asian students including ESL, a low ratio of students to native-speaking aides, mandatory hiring of special guidance counselors, and the creation of an Asian parents advocacy committee with a full-time coordinator.

CONCLUSION: RIGHTS OF LANGUAGE MINORITY STUDENTS

The previous discussion has highlighted the increasing number of court opinions related to language minority pupils over the last two decades. These opinions have in turn generated standards for the educational treatment of this population of students. At a national level, this legal standing stems from court opinions specifically interpreting Section 1703 (f) of the 1974 U.S. Equal Educational Opportunity Act. The courts have consistently refused to invoke a corollary interpretation regarding educational treatment using the Fourteenth Amendment to the U.S. Constitution. It is evident that litigation has increased (and is likely to continue) and has been an avenue of educational program reform that has produced significant changes in educational programs for language minority students. However, like almost all litigation, it has been a long (range of 4-13 years in court prior to an operational decision) and often highly complicated and resource-consuming enterprise.

Nevertheless, the responsibilities of educational agencies have been established. Following, in a question-and-answer format, are some of these responsibilities. These are adapted from Roos (1984) and carry with them a caution that both federal and state legal authority which led to these guidelines are always subject to legislative change and modifications in court interpretation. However, they do represent a practical guide for understanding the legal status of language minority students and legal liability of those educational agencies that serve them.

Question

Is there a legally acceptable procedure for identifying language minority students in need of special instructional treatment?

Answer

Yes. The legal obligation is to identify all students who have problems speaking, understanding, reading or writing English due to a home language background other than English. In order to do this, a two-phase approach is common and acceptable. First, the parents are asked, through a Home Language Survey or on a registration form, whether a language other than English is utilized in the child's home. If the answer is affirmative, then the second phase is triggered. In the second phase, those students identified through the Home Language Survey are given an oral language proficiency test **and** an assessment of their reading and writing skills.

Question

Once identified, are there any minimal standards for the educational program provided to these students?

Answer

Yes. First, a number of courts have recognized that special training is necessary to equip a teacher to provide meaningful assistance to limited English proficient students. The teacher (and it is clear that it must be a teacher, not an aide) must have training in second-language acquisition techniques to teach English as a Second Language (ESL).

Secondly, the time spent on assisting the student must be sufficient to assure that he/she acquire English skills quickly enough to assure that his/her disadvantage in the English language classroom does not harden into a permanent educational disadvantage.

Question

Must students be provided with instruction in the student's native language as well as English?

Answer

At the present time, the federal obligation has not been construed to affirmatively compel such a program. As a practical matter, however, the federal mandate is such that a district would be well advised to offer such a program whenever it is possible.

The federal mandate is not fully satisfied by an ESL program. The mandate requires English language help **plus** programs to assure that the students are not substantively handicapped by any delay in learning English. To do this requires either a bilingual program which keeps the student up in his course work while learning English or a specifically designed compensatory program to address the educational loss suffered by any delay in providing understandable substantive instruction. Given these alternatives, the legally "safe" posture is to offer native language instruction whenever it can be done. Finally, it is legally necessary to provide the material resources necessary for the instructional components. The program must be reasonably designed to succeed. Without adequate resources, this requirement cannot be met.

Question

What minimal standards must be met if a bilingual program is to be offered?

Answer

The heart of a basic bilingual program is a teacher who can speak the language of the student as well as address the students' limited English proficiency. Thus, a district offering a bilingual program must take affirmative steps to match teachers with these characteristics. These might include allocating teachers with language skills to bilingual classrooms, and affirmative recruitment of bilingual teachers. Additionally, it requires the district to establish a formal system to assess teachers to insure that they have the prerequisite skills. Finally, where there are insufficient teachers, there must be a system to insure that teachers with most (but not all) of the skills are in bilingual classrooms, that those teachers are on a track to obtain the necessary skills, and that bilingual aides are hired whenever the teacher lacks the necessary language skills.

Question

Must there be standards for removal of a student from a program? What might these be?

Answer

There must be definite standards. These generally mirror the standards for determining whether a student is in need of special language services in the first place. Thus, objective evidence that the student can compete with his English-speaking peers without a lingering language disability is necessary.

Several common practices are unlawful. First, the establishment of an arbitrary cap on the amount of time a student can remain in a program fails to meet the requirement that all language minority students be assisted. Secondly, it is common to have programs terminate at a certain grade level (e.g. sixth grade). While programs may change to accommodate different realities, it is unlawful to deny a student access to a program merely because of his grade level.

Question

Must a district develop a design to monitor the success of its program?

Answer

Yes. The district is obligated to monitor the program **and** to make reasonable adjustments when the evidence would suggest that the program is not successful.

Monitoring is necessarily a two-part process. First, it is necessary to monitor the progress of students in the program to assure (a) that they are making reasonable progress toward learning English and (b) that the program is providing the student with substantive instruction comparable to English proficient pupils. Second, any assessment of the program must include a system to monitor the progress of students after they leave the program. The primary purpose of the program is to assure that the LEP students ultimately are able to compete on an equal footing with their English-speaking peers. This cannot be determined if such a post-reclassification monitoring system is absent.

Question

May a district deny services to a student because there are few students in the district who speak his language?

Answer

No. The 1974 Equal Educational Opportunity Act and subsequent court decisions make it clear that every student is entitled to a program that is reasonably designed to overcome any handicaps occasioned by his language. Numbers may, obviously, be considered to determine **how** to address the student's needs. They are not a proper consideration in determining **whether** a program should be provided.

Although reluctant, U.S. courts have played a significant role in shaping language minority education policy. They have addressed issues of student identification, program implementation, resource allocation, professional staffing, and program effectiveness. Moreover, they have obligated both local and state educational agencies to meet the needs of language minority students. Moreover, because the courts are not constrained by the numbers of affected constituents, they have provided a forum in which minority status is not disadvantageous and as such have protected the rights of language minority students. However, it has been a forum which is highly ritualized, extremely time and resource consuming, and always reluctant.

Chapter 5

FEDERAL INITIATIVES

THIS CHAPTER first briefly describes the history of bilingual schooling until 1968 when the first Bilingual Education Act was passed. The chapter then traces the evolution of federal legislation — the Bilingual Education Act of 1968 and the Amendments of 1974 and 1978 — and ends with a detailed account of the interplay of factors that led to the passage of the Bilingual Education Act of 1984. A note on the 1988 reauthorization is included also.

Many factors interplay to produce a specific policy. According to Hayes (1982), they include "contextual factors, including social, economic, demographic, political and ideological factors; the activities of both organized and unorganized constituencies; actors and institutions and their principles and ideas; the media; and research." All of these factors played a part in the process that led to the passage of the Bilingual Education Act and its subsequent reauthorizations.

PROGRAM HISTORY PRIOR TO 1984 REAUTHORIZATION

Federal bilingual education programs were established in 1968 by an amendment to the Elementary and Secondary Education Act of 1965 (Public Law 90-247). The amendment, called the Title VII Bilingual Education Program, is also known as the Bilingual Education Act (BEA). Before 1968 the history of bilingual education can be divided into two phases: pre-World War I and post 1960. Before World War I, three major languages predominated in bilingual public schools: French in Louisiana and parts of New England, Spanish in New Mexico, and German in the East and Midwest. Norwegian, Czech, Italian, Polish,

73

Dutch, and Lithuanian were also taught as part of the curriculum in areas with large concentrations of students from these countries (Anderson and Boyer, 1970). Private schools, many with religious affiliations, were also established and provided instruction in native languages. In addition, such American Indian tribes as the Choctows, Creeks, and Seminoles established and operated their own schools, and by 1852 the Cherokees served 1,100 students in twenty-one schools and two academies (Leibowitz, 1980). Between 1920 and 1960 bilingual schooling in the United States virtually disappeared, mostly as a result of isolationism and nationalism pervasive in the United States after World War I. The second period of public bilingual education began in the early sixties, when thousands of Cuban refugees settled around Miami in Dade County, Florida. To meet the needs of Cuban children, the Dade County public school system initiated a bilingual program in the first three grades of the Coral Way School. In the year before the passage of the Bilingual Education Act, a few locally supported bilingual programs had been started in other cities in Florida, Texas, New Mexico, Arizona, and California.

A combination of events created a context in which the Bilingual Education Act of 1968 could pass (Judd, 1978). First, the existence of public bilingual education set a precedent which could be used to legitimize bilingual education. Second, a number of studies had been done by 1967 concluding that bilinguals equaled or surpassed monolinguals on intelligence tests and in other areas of language usage and creativity (Lambert and Peal, 1962; Lerea and Kohut, 1961; Lewis and Lewis, 1965; Jacobs and Pierce, 1966). Third, there was a movement away from the melting-pot theory of assimilation toward the concept of cultural pluralism. Newcomers were not expected to give up their cultural identity to blend into an "American identity" but had a right to maintain their own culture. This new orientation was fueled by the emergence of the civil rights movement and the ethnic consciousness that accompanied it. Fourth, during the late 1950s and 1960s Americans began to "rediscover" poverty, and education was perceived as a means of reducing poverty. Fifth, the passage of the Bilingual Education Act was helped by the passage of the Elementary and Secondary Education Act of 1965 which legitimized federal intervention in elementary and secondary education targeted to poor, low-achieving students. Sixth, the fear of the spread of communism from Cuba encouraged the United States to establish more of a presence in Central and South America. This presence took the form of establishing more sympathetic relations

through the use of Spanish-speaking bilingual official and unofficial am-
bassadors. Seventh, there was an interest in developing U.S. foreign
language capability as a result of the renewed United States competition
with the Soviet Union after the Russian launching of *Sputnik*. This interest was embodied in the National Defense Education Act passed in
1958. Title VI and later Title XI emphasized the retention and expan-
sion of foreign language resources. Eighth, 1980 census data indicated
that the total Spanish-surnamed population had increased by more than
50 percent between 1950 and 1960: to 3,464,999 from 2,281,710 (Leibowitz, 1980). The federal government and individual states responded to
this increased constituency by creating committees and commissions.
Their findings indicated Spanish-speaking children were encountering
difficulty in school, and education was a primary concern for Hispanics.
Finally, a number of powerful interest groups became involved in sup-
porting specific aid for Spanish-speaking students, in part as a result of a
conference in Tucson, Arizona organized by the National Education Association (NEA) to discuss the conditions of Spanish speakers in the
Southwest. A report conducted under NEA auspices further highlighted
the educational problems facing Spanish-speaking students and advo-
cated specific programs for them, including transitional bilingual education, ESL, teaching the culture and history of Spanish speakers, and
hiring Spanish-speaking teachers and aides.

In January 1967, Senator Ralph Yarborough (D-TX) introduced
S.428, a bill to provide assistance to local education agencies to establish
bilingual programs for students whose native language was Spanish and
for whom English was a foreign language. Other members of Congress,
however, supported an expanded definition of the students to be served.
By September 1967, forty-nine different congressmen had sponsored at
least one piece of bilingual education legislation. Most of these bills
called for bilingual education for all non-English-speaking groups.
Moreover, before S.428 passed out of the Senate Committee on Labor
and Public Welfare, all non-English-speaking groups were included in
the scope of the Senate bill's funding.

The bill was able to pass during the Ninetieth Congress for several
reasons (Judd, 1978). President Johnson was determined to create a
"Great Society" and viewed education as an important means of alleviat-
ing poverty. Furthermore, his roots were in the Southwest and he was
sympathetic to legislation aiding Hispanics. Although Johnson initially
wanted to serve children from other linguistic groups through Title I of
the Elementary and Secondary Education Act of 1965, he agreed to sup-

port the bill when it incorporated a broader approach directed at serving children from environments where the dominant language was not English rather than only Hispanics and when he realized the bill had substantial congressional support. He was a strong president and able, with his long experience as a congressman, to enact most of the bills he promoted. The Senate was controlled by the Democrats who supported Johnson's domestic policy. Although the House was controlled by a conservative coalition of southern Democrats and Republicans, it did not vote on the Bilingual Education Act separately but as one of many amendments to the Elementary and Secondary Education Act. Accordingly on January 2, 1968, President Johnson was able to sign the bill into law, and bilingual education became a federal policy for the first time in the history of the United States. No funds were appropriated in FY 1968, and of the $30 million authorized in FY 1969, $7.5 million was appropriated.

The BEA was intended as a demonstration program designed to meet the educational needs of low-income, limited-English-speaking children. Upon application, grants could be awarded to local educational agencies, institutions of higher education, or regional research facilities to: (a) develop and operate bilingual education programs, native history and culture programs, early childhood education programs, adult education programs, and programs to train bilingual aides; (b) make efforts to attract and retain as teachers individuals from non-English-speaking backgrounds; and (c) establish cooperation between the home and the school.

Four major reauthorizations of the BEA have occurred since 1968 — in 1974, 1978, 1984, and 1988. Appropriations grew from $58.4 million in FY 1974 to a high of $167 million in FY 1980, and are currently $146.6 million for FY 1988. As a consequence of the 1974 amendments (Public Law 93-380), a bilingual education program was defined for the first time as "instruction given in, and study of English, and to the extent necessary to allow a child to progress effectively through the education system, the native language" (Schneider, 1976, pp. 436-437). The goal of bilingual education continued to be a transition to English rather than maintenance of the native language. Children no longer had to be low income to participate. Two new programs were funded: (a) a graduate fellowship program for persons interested in training teachers for bilingual education programs, and (b) a program for the development, assessment, and dissemination of classroom materials.

In the Bilingual Education Amendments of 1978 (Public Law 95-561), program eligibility was expanded to include limited-English-proficient students with limited proficiency in academic skills as well as oral language. Bilingual education specialists had found that oral proficiency was not enough to prevent LEP students from failing in mainstream classes. Parents were given a greater role in program planning and operation in order to enable them to monitor program effectiveness and make programs more responsive to community needs. Teachers were required to be proficient in both English and the native language of the children in the program. Capacity building was encouraged; grant recipients were required to demonstrate how they would continue the program when federal funds were withdrawn (Congressional Research Service, 1984).

In 1981, the Reagan administration attempted to fold Title VII into the Chapter 2 block grant. Chapter 2 repealed 29 categorical programs and provided states with a single authorization of grants for use primarily at the local level for basic skills development, educational improvement and support services, and special projects. However, due to pressure from the Congressional Hispanic Caucus and Secretary of Education Bell, Title VII was never incorporated into the Chapter 2 block grant and remained a categorical program. The secretary maintained that a block grant would not effectively distribute funds, because limited-English-proficient students were unevenly distributed geographically. Even though the BEA was not folded into Chapter 2, its funding ceiling was reduced. The Omnibus Budget Reconciliation Act of 1981 reduced the authorization ceiling from $350 million to $139.97 million and reauthorized bilingual education programs for one year. The Technical Amendments to the Education Consolidation and Improvement Act of 1981 promulgated in 1983 amended the authorization period and extended Title VII through fiscal year 1984.

BILINGUAL EDUCATION ACT OF 1984

Beginning in January of 1983, a Department of Education interagency group composed of representatives from the Office of Bilingual Education, the Office of Planning, Budget, and Evaluation (OPBE), the Office of Civil Rights, and the Inspector General's Office met almost every week until mid March to draft amendments to the BEA. Five major changes were proposed: (a) The definition of bilingual education in the act would be broadened to include a range of instructional approaches that did not require instruction in the child's native language. Under the current act, a district had to use the child's native language in the instructional program. A report prepared by OPBE on the effectiveness of bilingual education programs (Baker and de Kanter, 1981) concluded that transitional bilingual education should not be the only approach for instructing language minority students, since there is no firm evidence that transitional bilingual education is uniquely effective in raising language minority students' performance in English and in non-language subject areas (as compared with submersion, English as a Second Language, or immersion). In addition, the Department of Education interagency group felt that certain child and classroom factors might make the use of native language instruction infeasible. For example, children whose proficiency in English was stronger than their native language proficiency might benefit more from English-only instruction. In some districts, small numbers of LEP students from multiple language groups make bilingual programs difficult to implement—in part because there are too few students in each group and because qualified teachers are unavailable. (b) Basic grants in school districts would be focused on building the capacity of the district to continue to serve LEP students when federal funds are withdrawn. As such, districts could only receive a total of five years of federal funding. Under current law, districts were eligible to apply for a new three-year grant if they were going to work with different grade levels or languages or schools in the district. The Department of Education Budget Office had discovered that 284 districts (41%) that had received Title VII funds had received federal aid for six or more years; 105 districts had received support for ten years or more. (c) Title VII funds would be targeted on programs that served limited-English-proficient children whose usual language was not English. The interagency team felt that many children who spoke English better than their native language were being served by Title VII. They based their estimate of number of LEP students on a study, "Size of the Eligible Language-Minority-Population" by Robert Barnes, reported in an OPBE policy paper (Birman and Ginsburg, 1981). Barnes reported that 16 percent of the 3.6 million estimated LEP students use English as their only language and another 40 percent use English as their usual language. (d) The role of state educational agencies (SEAs) would be strengthened by providing financial support to SEAs for activities to improve bilingual education and to review and coordinate bilingual education programs. Under the current act, states received only a limited amount of funding to coordinate technical assistance for bilingual programs. Giving the states more program responsibility was in keeping with the Reagan administration's agenda of decentralization. (e) Vocational projects for providing out-of-school youth with vocational education would be authorized under the Bilingual Education Act. Under current law, the program was authorized under the Vocational Education Act but administered by the Office of Bilingual Education and Minority Language Affairs (OBEMLA) and appropriated under the Bilingual Education appropriation. The changes made legislative authority consistent with program and budget authority.

These recommended changes were incorporated into H.R. 2682, the Bilingual Education Improvement Act of 1983, which was introduced on April 21, 1983 by two congressmen, Mr. Erlenborn (R-IL) and Mr. Goodling (R-PA). This bill never received as much as a hearing, although a part of it eventually was incorporated into the Bilingual Education Act of 1984: A 4 percent set-aside was provided for special alternative programs that did not require use of the native language for instruction, and states were authorized to provide services besides technical assistance and could not receive less than $50,000 for any fiscal year.

Several national organizations played a major role in shaping the final bill adopted by Congress (the Bilingual Education Act of the Education Amendments of 1984), because there was a relative lack of practical experience and expertise with bilingual education among Washington policymakers who were sympathetic to bilingual education (Orum, 1984). These national organizations had long played an educational and technical assistance role and had provided policymakers with fact-based information about the mechanics of bilingual education, the characteristics of the client population, and the problems faced by LEP communities. When it came time to reauthorize Title VII, congressional staff turned to several of these organizations to provide assistance in drafting legislation that took into account the needs of service providers and recipients. Although a variety of organizations provided policy suggestions, two of these organizations — the National Association for Bilingual Education (NABE), and The National Council of La Raza (NCLR) — played a key role in coordinating the assistance and in helping members of Congress draft legislation.

The development of legislative proposals was based on a strong foundation of policy analysis conducted in 1981, 1982, and 1983 by the National Council of La Raza, the National Association for Bilingual Education, and the Center for Hispanic Educational Leadership. NCLR's

Education Policy Analysis Component, together with the Center for Research and Advanced Studies at George Mason University, initiated a policy analysis project early in 1981 to explore policy options for the reauthorization of the federal Bilingual Education Act. At the time, Title VII was due to be reauthorized in 1983. It was anticipated that the reauthorization process would resemble the previous reauthorizations in 1974 and 1978, with hearings held sometime in 1982, and opportunity for public comment, testimony and other input into proposed amendments.

The NCLR policy analysis project was developed on the assumption that Title VII could be strengthened in a variety of ways in response to changing needs and as a result of research and experience gained since the last program reauthorization. The project assumed that both service providers (i.e. teachers, administrators, trainers, etc.) and service recipients (including students, parents and community members) should participate in discussions of policy options. Furthermore, the project drew on the resources of a coalition of organizations representing various language minority populations concerned about education. The project sponsored a series of meetings around the country and prepared a series of issue-option papers to further explore issues most commonly raised. NCLR leadership also participated in a conference of leaders in bilingual and foreign language instruction, convened by the Edward W. Hazen Foundation, to discuss the future of bilingual education and submit recommendations to Secretary of Education Bell. The end result of the reauthorization policy analysis project was a collection of issue papers analyzing major issues and suggested policy options. Issues raised included:

1. The level of specificity needed in the legislation to increase program accountability;
2. The possibility of expanding Title VII to include other related education areas such as foreign languages and English as a Second Language (ESL);
3. The feasibility and possible content of a national language policy;
4. The necessity for targeting provisions in the legislation;
5. Standards of minimum competency for bilingual teachers;
6. The possibility of encouraging two-way bilingual education programs (programs involving children whose native language is English) as well as methods to involve limited-English-proficient parents in helping their children in school;
7. The most beneficial mix of Title VII activities (i.e. capacity-

building activities, training projects, research, and grants for bilingual programs in the schools); and

8. The role of the cultural heritage aspects of the legislation.

The NCLR issues and options were presented at the 1982 meeting of
the National Association for Bilingual Education. The session was well
attended and the debate was spirited. The consensus was that bilingual
education has something valuable to offer to all children, and should be
strengthened by improving the federal bilingual education effort, expanding to cooperate with personnel and organizations in related fields,
and using higher competency standards for personnel. There were also
many recommendations that the federal legislation specify program,
data collection, and evaluation requirements in greater detail in order to
promote greater program accountability. Despite the feeling that the legislation should be improved, most participants were also hesitant to
amend the Title VII legislation, feeling that the climate created by congressional and administration proposals made any change risky and advocating amendments would only strengthen the efforts to kill the
program.

During 1981, NABE's Sociopolitical Concerns Committee conducted
its own survey, polling NABE members around the country concerning
possible changes in Title VII. The committee's conclusion, reported at
another session of the organization's 1982 annual conference, was that
the existing structure of Title VII was adequate to deal with any changing needs or political challenges, and that the legislation should be left
intact. It recommended that efforts be directed at better explaining Title
VII to the Congress and the public, countering attempts to legislatively
weaken bilingual education, and ensuring that Title VII be reauthorized
in its existing form. These recommendations also reflected the concern
that proposing amendments at that time might easily play into the hands
of those who wished to end or weaken the program.

In 1982 and much of 1983, while reacting to proposed amendments
and editorials advocating the abolition of bilingual education, NCLR
and NABE devoted substantial efforts to articulating their position on
bilingual education. NCLR prepared a briefing paper for congressional
staff and the public, entitled, "Beyond the Myths: Title VII and Bilingual Education in the United States," and published and disseminated a
document offering short answers to common questions about bilingual
education. Upon request, NCLR and other interested organizations—
most commonly NABE, the Mexican American Legal Defense and

Education Fund (MALDEF), and the League of United Latin American Citizens (LULAC)—also analyzed proposed amendments to Title VII, submitted testimony, and provided ongoing reports to the National Advisory Committee on Bilingual Education. NABE, which had previously been only sporadically represented in Washington, D.C., reallocated its resources and hired a legislative counsel to monitor legislative proposals and provide the association's perspective in federal policy discussions of bilingual education.

The bill's eventual sponsors, Congressmen Kildee (D-MI) and Corrada (N.P.-PR), indicated they wanted new bilingual education legislation that would incorporate all that had been learned through experience in the field and research. As a consequence, policy analysis efforts continued with the goal of crafting a new bilingual education bill. In addition to the heavy involvement of NCLR, their affiliates, and other Hispanic organizations, successful efforts were made to secure the involvement of American Indians, Asian Americans, Pacific Islanders, Arab Americans and other language minority groups. Many NCLR board members, affiliates, and members of NCLR's education network criticized a series of drafts—adding, deleting, developing, and advising.

There was tremendous utility if not speed in the participation of so many diverse groups. Some concepts, which had seemed a good idea from a Washington perspective, were eliminated when practitioners and local community members questioned their efficacy. Some approaches which were sensible in certain communities did not adapt well to others. Community members and organizations provided an important perspective on the needs of parents and out-of-school family members and on the key role that community-based organizations can play in education. Teachers highlighted the need for retraining and in-service education; administrators offered valuable advice about program organization, management, and procedures. Researchers highlighted areas in which additional study was urgently needed, and business people spoke of the need for a work force—both literate and bilingual. Congressional staff provided analyses of the political feasibility of various options. The common call from all participants was for a program with increased accountability; better trained teachers; and that provided greater attention to full English language proficiency, literacy, and subject mastery and increased community involvement. After several months that entailed multiple drafts and revisions and the concerted efforts of many people, the legislation was completed. It was not a "perfect bill," but it represented the consensus of a broad cross section of involved individuals and organizations, and represented an effort to respond to legitimate criticisms of the previous program.

The bill met with the approval of Congressmen Kildee and Corrada, who announced their intention to introduce the proposal as legislation. They set out the general themes of the proposed bill in a letter to their colleagues, inviting cosponsors. Within a few days, 57 members of Congress responded affirmatively; included was the entire congressional Hispanic caucus. The bill was introduced on March 22, 1984 as H.R. 5231, The Academic Equity and Excellence through Bilingual Education Act.

Hearings on H.R. 5231 were held on March 27, 1984 in the House Subcommittee on Elementary, Secondary, and Vocational Education. Witnesses from the National Association for Bilingual Education, the California State Department of Education, the National School Boards Association, and the Michigan State Board of Education testified on behalf of the legislation. Former Senator S.I. Hayakawa, honorary chairman of U.S. English, a group advocating the repeal of the bilingual provisions of the Voting Rights Act and a constitutional amendment to establish English as the official language of the country, testified in opposition to the bill.

The congressional Hispanic caucus scheduled speeches by caucus and non-caucus members on the House floor on April 3, 1984 to educate their colleagues on the needs of limited-English-proficient children, the workings of bilingual programs, and the features of the Kildee-Corrada bill. Sixteen members of the House spoke or inserted material into the April third *Congressional Record.*

During the subcommittee hearings on H.R. 5231, Congressman Steve Bartlett (R-TX) had advised cosponsors Kildee and Corrada of his support for bilingual education but also of this concerns about the need for greater program flexibility in the legislation. He offered his assistance and that of Congressman John McCain (R-AZ) to work with members Kildee and Corrada to fashion amendments to expand the flexibility in the bill. Both Representatives Bartlett and McCain represented congressional districts with significant numbers of the limited-English-proficient population. LULAC staff provided both members with detailed information on bilingual education and facilitated conversations between the congressmen and their language minority constituents. After the hearings, several meetings took place between Congressmen Kildee, Corrada, Bartlett, and McCain to work on a bipartisan compromise which would allow for other program options but retain an adequate level of support for bilingual programs. Despite long hours of negotiation and what all agreed had been a good-faith effort, they were unable to reach agreement on amendments.

On April 24, the subcommittee met to discuss and amend ("markup") H.R. 11, legislation introduced by Chairman Carl Perkins (D-KY), to provide simple extensions for a variety of federal education programs, including the previous Bilingual Education Act. During the process of discussing and amending various provisions of the bill, the subcommittee agreed to substitute H.R. 5231 for the provisions in H.R. 11 which would have reauthorized the current Bilingual Education Act. Discussion and votes at this markup were divided along party lines.

Republican members of the subcommittee voiced their opposition to the legislation's continued emphasis on bilingual education programs and to the lack of funding opportunities for monolingual English approaches such as English-as-a-Second-Language and structured immersion programs. Some members pointed out that there were schools which were composed of such a diversity of language groups or had such a shortage of bilingual teachers that bilingual programs would not be possible. Some charged that the legislation-mandated curriculum was overly intrusive. Other Republican members sharply attacked the efficacy of bilingual education programs, advocating instead the use of English immersion programs. Congressmen Kildee, Corrada, and other Democratic members acknowledged concerns about the administrative impracticality of programs in some districts, but pointed out that the act was currently underfunded and could not meet the existing need for bilingual education. They urged that funds for the establishment of other types of programs be newly appropriated monies, not funds taken away from bilingual education. They also pointed out that there were very few structured immersion programs, that little research existed to demonstrate their effectiveness, and cautioned against federal support for programs which may be disguised versions of "sink-or-swim" schooling.

Ultimately, the subcommittee rejected an amendment introduced by Representative Bill Goodling (R-PA), which incorporated most of the features of the Reagan administration's previous bilingual education amendments, and an amendment proposed by Representative Steve Bartlett (R-TX) which would have earmarked 15 percent of the funds in H.R. 5231 for "special alternative instructional programs." These programs would not have been required to use the child's native language for any instructional purposes and therefore would have dramatically changed the nature of the legislation. After much detailed discussion between the members of Congress, their staff members, and technical assistance provided by NCLR, NABE, MALDEF, and LULAC, the members arrived at a mutually acceptable bipartisan compromise which was adopted on May 2, when the House Education and Labor Committee met to examine the subcommittee's version of H.R. 11.

The amendments expanded the bilingual education provisions of H.R. 11 to include some funding for the Special Alternative Instructional Programs previously proposed by Congressman Bartlett. Under the Agreement, 4 percent of the funds then available for Title VII (approximately $140 million) would be set aside for alternative programs. The alternative programs would be required to use "specially designed curricula and [be] appropriate for the particular linguistic and instructional needs of the children enrolled [and provide] structured English language instruction and special instructional services which would allow a child to achieve competence in the English language and to meet grade-promotion and graduation standards." The amendments also specified that 4 percent of the total Title VII appropriation when $140 million or under, or 50 percent of newly appropriated monies (over $140 million) would be used for the Special Alternative Instruction Programs, subject to limitation of 10 percent of the bill's total funding. Additionally, the amendments would allow the secretary of education to give preference to those alternative program areas in which the implementation of bilingual education was administratively impractical, due to small numbers of students from any given language or the unavailability of qualified bilingual teachers.

After committee approval, the legislation proceeded to the House floor. On July 25, the House took up the bilingual education provisions of H.R. 11. After the adoption of amendments proposed by Congressman Goodling, designed to increase parental choice in program placement and allow the funding of exemplary Special Alternative Instructional Programs, the title of the bill dealing with bilingual education was passed by voice vote. On July 26, the House approved the entire bill, placed authorization caps on the funding for included programs, and added an amendment authorizing silent prayer in the public schools. The House then attached H.R. 11 to the Senate's Adult Education Bill, S.2496, and sent the measure to the Senate for approval. Despite the interest of several senators, time constraints in the Senate had prohibited the introduction of companion bilingual education legislation in the Senate.

The Senate, divided on the issue of school prayer and several programs included in the omnibus bill, balked at approving this new version of S.2496. Discussions lagged over the summer and came to a temporary standstill after the unexpected death of House Committee Chairman Perkins in August. Conferees were appointed in the fall so that the House and Senate could negotiate a final version of the bill in the conference committee. After approving an amendment limiting the authority of the secretary of education to further define the programs defined in the act by regulation, and reducing the authorization period from five to four years, the conference committee approved the bilingual education provisions of the bill. Discussions and compromises on other sections of the legislation were more extensive. The school prayer amendment was dropped at the insistence of the Senate and some programs were modified, but accord was eventually reached, and all members of the conference committee signed the report that recommended passage of the legislation.

On October 3, the Senate approved the conference report on S.2496; the House followed suit on October 4. The bill was sent to President Reagan for signature and was signed into law as P.L. 98-511 on October 19, 1984. President Reagan issued a statement announcing the signing of the legislation and noted his support for the bipartisan Bilingual Education Act. Specifically, he stated:

> I am especially pleased that the amendments to the Bilingual Education Act allow some flexibility for school districts to use Federal funds for the many proven alternatives to the traditional methods in bilingual education that they believe are better suited to helping their limited English speaking students learn English. In the future, I hope to work with the Congress to further expand this much needed flexibility.

PROGRAM STRUCTURE

The Bilingual Education Act of the Education Amendments of 1984 reauthorized the Bilingual Education Act from FY 1985 through FY 1988. There are four parts to the act (Stein, 1985). Part A provides 60 percent of the act's funds for a wide variety of education programs: **Transitional Bilingual Educational Programs** provide native language instruction to the extent necessary to enable a child to meet promotion and graduation requirements. Transitional programs must also contain a structured English language component. **Special Alternative Instructional Programs** need not use a child's native language but must have specifically designed curricula, must be appropriate for the particular linguistic and instructional needs of the children, and must provide structured English language instruction and special instructional services to enable a child to achieve competence in English and meet grade-promotion and graduation standards. **Developmental Bilingual Education Programs** are composed of equal numbers of limited-English-proficient and fluent English-speaking children and are designed to enable all children to achieve competence in English and a second language. **Academic Excellence Programs** are programs that have already established a record of providing effective instruction, and grants are used to strengthen and use such programs for demonstration. **Family English Literacy Programs** help parents and out-of-school family members of limited-English-proficient children to acquire competence in the English language and instruct them on how to facilitate their children's educational achievement. Funds also are available for bilingual preschool and special education programs, for Indian children, for students in Puerto Rico, and for projects to develop teaching materials in languages where commercially produced materials are unavailable.

Part B provides funds for (a) collecting data on the number of limited-English-proficient people in a given area and the educational services available to them; (b) evaluating the operation and effectiveness of educational programs assisted by the act; (c) conducting research to improve the effectiveness of bilingual educational programs; and (d) operating a clearinghouse to collect, analyze, and disseminate information about bilingual education and related programs. Proposals for Part B funds may be submitted by institutions of higher education, private for-profit and non-profit organizations, state and local educational agencies, and individuals.

Part C funds are used for training and retraining teachers; fellowships for advanced studies in bilingual education; assistance to schools of education to encourage reform, innovation, and improvement in applicable education curricula in graduate education; in the recruitment and retention of higher education and graduate school faculties related to bilingual education; and the provision of technical assistance to school districts implementing bilingual education programs.

Part D establishes an Office of Bilingual Education and Minority-Language Affairs (OBEMLA) to be headed by a director, and a National Advisory and Coordinating Council on Bilingual Education to advise the director and help prepare reports, regulations, research agendas, and policies.

SUMMARY

That the bill was able to become a law was a consequence of the interplay of a number of factors. First, the political context was propitious. The House of Representatives was controlled by the Democrats. Two Democrats on the House Elementary, Secondary, and Vocational Education Subcommittee were willing to sponsor legislation drafted in large part by bilingual education advocates. Two Republicans were willing to sponsor a compromise version of the bill, acceptable to the bilingual education advocacy community. Both of these Republican congressmen were from states heavily populated by Hispanics. Both had statewide ambitions and knew they would eventually become involved in this issue. They realized the importance of the Hispanic constituency for the Republican Party. The president signed the bill a month before the presidential election, in part because he wanted to court the Hispanic vote. Second, many language minority groups had been involved in conceptualizing and drafting legislation and were actively engaged in lobbying their congressmen. Third, that they were so actively engaged was in large measure a consequence of two very effective Washington-based policy analysts representing NABE and La Raza. These analysts had drafted the legislation with the help of many individuals and groups and were able to shepherd the legislation through Congress, partly because of broad-based field support and partly because they had extensive expertise in the area of language minority education. Finally, both research and the media played a role in the passage of the act, but because there were articles and publicity both supportive of bilingual education and opposed to it, one point of view balanced out the other, and in the end neither research nor publicity influenced the political process.

RECENT LEGISLATIVE ACTIVITY

At the time this chapter is being written, the Bilingual Education Act is again being reauthorized. This time around the House Education and Labor Committee Democrats compromised in return for a Republican promise of fast passage of H.R. 5, a bill to revise and extend through 1993 all federal elementary, secondary, and adult education programs of which the BEA is a part.

On March 23, 1987, House Education and Labor Chairman Augustus F. Hawkins (D-CA) introduced H.R. 1755 with fellow committee members Dale Kildee (D-MI), Mathew Martinez (D-CA) and Bill Richardson (D-NM). The bill proposed a series of minor adjustments to the Bilingual Education Act. In brief, it:

- Reauthorized Title VII through FY 1993 and increased the FY 1988 authorization level to $246 million;
- Expanded program flexibility by replacing the current 6-month preservice requirement for all Part A grants with a provision permitting grantees to engage exclusively in preservice activities during the first 12 months of a Part A grant; and included developmental bilingual education programs within the existing funding reservation (75% of Part A Grants) for transitional bilingual education;
- Encouraged greater state responsibility by increasing the minimum state grant from $50,000 to $75,000, and eliminating NACCBE and requiring OBEMLA to work directly with state directors of bilingual education in coordinating Title VII policies and programs;
- Assured parental participation by strengthening and continuing the Parent Advisory Committees, and by requiring that information provided to parents pursuant to Title VII be in a language and form they understand;
- Preserved existing fund reservation (25% of all Title VII appropriations) for training and retraining and required a minimum of 500 fellowships per year.

During April 7-9, H.R. 5 was marked up in the House Elementary, Secondary and Vocational Education Subcommittee. During the markup, the subcommittee approved the incorporation of H.R. 1755, the Bilingual Education Act, into H.R. 5. In addition, Steve Bartlett (R-TX) offered an amendment to increase the relative proportion of Title VII funds available for English-only instructional programs from 10 percent of total act appropriations to 25 percent of Part A appropriations. The amendment also provided that grants for transitional bilingual education, developmental bilingual education, and special alternative instructional programs "shall include curriculums designed to achieve competence in the English language within three years while allowing the child to meet grade-promotion and graduation standards." There was considerable debate on the amendments and no agreement. Chairman Hawkins finally suggested that members use the week-long Easter district work period to resolve their differences.

The compromise that was worked out by Dale Kildee (D-MI) and Steve Bartlett (R-TX) during full Education and Labor Committee markup on April 22, 1987 included the following components: an authorization of $246 million in fiscal year 1988 and such sums as necessary thereafter; the removal of the ceiling on grants to English-only programs. Under current law, only 4 percent of annual appropriations up to $140 million can be earmarked for English-only programs plus half of any additional funds, but no more than 10 percent of the total. The new bill requires that at least 4 percent of current funding be reserved for English-only programs and eliminates the 10 percent ceiling on additional funds; a decrease in the minimum amount for teacher training from 25 to 20 percent; a requirement that native language programs and teacher-training programs receive at least as much in any fiscal year as was appropriated in fiscal 1987 ($81.6 million for native language programs and $33.6 million for teacher-training programs); the establishment of a new formula for distributing funds if appropriations exceed fiscal 1987 levels. For amounts above the fiscal 1987 funding level, native language instruction programs and teacher training will receive enough additional money to cover the cost of inflation as measured by the consumer price index. Of the remaining amount, not less than 70 percent and not more than 75 percent of new funds must go to English-only programs. The final 25 percent must go to native language programs, with one million dollars reserved for developmental bilingual programs. The bill passed the House in June 1987 without further amendments to the Bilingual Education Act.

In the Senate, Dan Quayle (R-IN) introduced a bill in 1986 that would have removed the current provisions that limit spending for English-only programs. In 1987, Senator Quayle introduced another bill, S.857, to reserve 25 percent of funds for Special Alternative Instructional Programs (SAIP) that do not require native language use. At the request of Senator Claiborne Pell (D-RI), chairman of the Education, Arts, and the Humanities Subcommittee, Senator Quayle added another provision to limit a student's enrollment in transitional, developmental, or English-only programs to three years. The Labor and Human Resources Committee postponed a decision on the set-aside for SAIP until the Government Accounting Office could provide an estimate of the percentage of LEP children who are so scattered that schools cannot feasibly provide a bilingual education program for them. Based on an estimate by the Government Accounting Office that between 22 and 28 percent of LEP children were in low concentrations by language minority group, Senators Pell and Quayle, supported by members of the Senate Committee on Labor and Human Resources, offered a compromise to S.857. Up to 25 percent of Part A funds could be used for Special Alternative Instructional Programs. New money for alternative programs would first go to school districts where many languages are spoken or where there are not enough qualified bilingual teachers. The 75 percent reservation of Part A funds for transitional programs was retained. Part A programs, other than TBE or SAIP, could be funded from either the 25 or the 75 percent reservation. "Hold-harmless" language was also incorporated into the compromise to ensure that no changes would be made in the terms, conditions, or negotiated levels of grants made in fiscal year 1987. Students could be enrolled in the TBE or SAIP programs for a fourth or fifth year if a comprehensive evaluation indicated that the student's level of English proficiency was impeding his or her academic progress.

This compromise became S.1238, sponsored by Chairman of the Labor and Human Resources Committee, Edward Kennedy (D-MA). Before S.1238 was incorporated into S.373, the Omnibus Elementary and Secondary Education Bill, subcommittee staff made one more change—the elimination of the National Advisory and Coordinating Council of Bilingual Education—because of the controversy it had generated over the past few years. S.373 set the following authorization levels: $168 million for FY 1987; $177 million for FY 1990; $185 million for FY 1991; $195 million for FY 1992; and $200 million for FY 1993. It provided separate authorization levels for state grants for state data collection, evaluation, and research: $8 million for FY 1989 and FY 1990; $9 million for FY 1991 and FY 1992; and $10 million for FY 1993.

When the bill reached the Senate floor, Senator Steve Symms (R-ID) offered an amendment that "no action taken may involve the assignment of students to any federally assisted education program merely on the basis of the surname of such student." He also offered a "sense of the Senate" resolution providing that if a state requires a written authorization from parents to enroll a student in a bilingual education program, the state's authorization form should provide an opportunity for the parents to express either approval or disapproval of such enrollment. The Senate approved both amendments by voice vote. S.373 passed the Senate on December 2, 1987.

House and Senate conferees approved the $7.5 billion comprehensive school-aid authorization (H.R. 5) on March 31, 1988. Bilingual education provisions:

- Increase the bill's authorization level to $200 million for FY 1989 and such sums as necessary for each remaining year through FY 1993;
- Require that Part A grants receive a minimum of 60% of the total appropriation. Transitional Bilingual Education Programs must receive a minimum of 75% of Part A funds. Special Alternative Instruction Programs can receive up to 25% of Part A funds. Developmental Bilingual Education Programs, Programs of Academic Excellence, Family English Literacy Programs and Programs for Special Populations may be funded from either the 75% for Transitional Programs or from the 25% for Special Alternative Programs. There is no minimum or maximum allocation for Part B Data Collection, Evaluation and Research. Part C Training Programs must receive 25% of the total appropriation. Recipients of transitional education grants in FY 1987 will continue to receive at least as much through the remainder of existing contracts.
- Allow students to be enrolled in TBE or SAIP programs for a fourth or fifth year only if teachers and school personnel familiar with the students' overall academic progress have conducted an evaluation. The results of the evaluation must be made available to students' parents. The fourth and fifth year emphasis must be on English acquisition;
- Eliminate the Secretary's ability to further define any terms in the Act through regulation;
- Require that every effort shall be made to provide information to parents in a language and form they understand;
- Allow enrollment in the Family English Literacy Program to fulfill the Immigration Reform Act's requirements for achieving an understanding of English and United States government and history;
- Prohibit federal employees from reading and scoring applications made to the Department of Education. State Bilingual Education directors will now nominate readers; and
- Eliminate Senator Symms "Sense of the Senate resolution."

By a voice vote on April 20, 1988, the Senate passed H.R. 5, which the House overwhelmingly approved 397-1 the day before. President Reagan signed the bill into law on April 26, 1988.

Chapter 6

STATE INITIATIVES

OVERVIEW OF STATE LEGISLATION

EACH STATE and territory defines its own approach to educating language minority children. Table A (NCBE Forum, 1986) presents state profiles for 1984-85. One way to categorize these approaches is to examine state legislative requirements or lack thereof. In 1984-85, twelve states and Guam had legislation that mandated special educational services for limited-English-proficient students. Twelve other states, American Samoa, and the Virgin Islands passed legislation that allowed, but did not require, the programs for limited-English-proficient students described in the legislation. One state, West Virginia, prohibited special services. Twenty-six states, the Northern Marianas, Puerto Rico, and the Trust Territory of the Pacific had no legislation.

Tables B and C (NCBE, 1986) provide a summary of legislative provisions. As these tables indicate, a variety of legislative provisions can be incorporated into each law. States may either mandate or recommend that they be part of the law. Such provisions include criteria for program eligibility and program exit; the kind of programs available for language minority children (transitional, maintenance, ESL, cultural component); and the evaluation of students in the programs, including minimum competency testing, yearly and/or biyearly evaluations. Other provisions define the mix of students in such programs, either by prohibiting segregation or permitting the inclusion of monolingual English speakers in the program. Finally, a few states have a division responsible for monitoring the enforcement of state law.

TABLE A

Educating the LEP Student: 1984-85 State Profiles

State or Territory	Legislation[1] Mandates	Permits	Prohibits BE	No Statute	Teacher Certif.[2] Bilingual Education	ESL	Title VII Funding[3]
Alabama				✔			$ 0
Alaska	✔						1,380,763
Arizona	✔				✔	✔	2,148,151
Arkansas				✔			258,000
California	✔				✔	✔	23,241,751
Colorado		✔			✔		1,848,737
Connecticut	✔						1,085,098
Delaware				✔	✔		0
D.C.				✔	✔	✔	1,911,702
Florida				✔	✔	✔	4,064,533
Georgia				✔			101,435
Hawaii				✔		✔	1,416,156
Idaho				✔			468,569
Illinois	✔				✔	✔	3,479,641
Indiana		✔					668,758
Iowa	✔						525,764
Kansas		✔					3,316
Kentucky				✔		✔	308,357
Louisiana				✔		✔	1,703,195
Maine		✔					418,219
Maryland		✔					267,809
Massachusetts	✔				✔	✔	4,105,023
Michigan	✔				✔		5,880,876
Minnesota		✔			✔	✔	1,644,535
Mississippi				✔			305,280
Missouri				✔			120,000
Montana				✔			1,632,103
Nebraska				✔	✔	✔	267,971
Nevada				✔		✔	147,204
New Hampshire		✔			✔	✔	0
New Jersey	✔				✔	✔	2,236,909
New Mexico		✔			✔	✔	4,642,232
New York		✔			✔	✔	22,034,517
North Carolina				✔		✔	$ 346,996
North Dakota				✔			1,690,083
Ohio				✔	✔	✔	1,564,612
Oklahoma				✔			2,792,391
Oregon		✔					1,673,266
Pennsylvania				✔			1,368,279
Rhode Island		✔			✔	✔	1,518,701
South Carolina				✔			13,000
South Dakota		✔					1,269,409
Tennessee				✔		✔	472,685
Texas	✔				✔	✔	11,316,342
Utah		✔					1,422,586
Vermont				✔	✔		508,476
Virginia				✔		✔	498,117
Washington	✔				✔	✔	1,876,689
West Virginia			✔				0
Wisconsin	✔				✔	✔	598,570
Wyoming				✔			305,789
Amer Samoa		✔			✔		170,000
Guam	✔				✔		607,433
N. Marianas				✔			0
Puerto Rico				✔		✔	1,992,388
Tr Terr of Pacific				✔			841,104
Virgin Islands		✔					83,508

1. Whether state legislation mandates, permits, or prohibits special educational services for limited-English-proficient (LEP) students. e.g., transitional bilingual education (TBE). English as a second language (ESL), immersion, and maintenance programs. For further information on individual states, contact NCBE.
2. Whether state offers teaching certification in Bilingual Education.
3. Federal funding under Title VII of the Bilingual Education Act as amended.

Source: Compiled from information provided by each SEA listed.

Source: U.S. Department of Education, National Clearinghouse for Bilingual Education. (1986) Forum, IX, 3.

TABLE B

Summary of Provisions Contained in State Bilingual Instruction/Education Legislation for States Mandating Special Instructional Services

STATE	IEP	Transitional	Language Maintenance	ESL	Provision of LEP Status	No Segregation	Include Monolingual Speakers	Entry/Exit Criteria	Minimum Competency Testing	Student Evaluation	Annual Exam in English	Parental Consent	Parental/Community Involvement	Cultural Component	Outline of Methodology	State Advisory Council	Availability of State Funds	Staff Development Funds	Enforcement of Legislation
AK		X	X	X	X			X		X		X	X	X	X		X	X	X
AZ	X	X	X	X	X			X	X	X		Notify		X					X
CA		X			X	X	X	X		X		X	X	X			X	X	X
CT		X		X	X	X		X		X		X				X	X	X	X
IL		X			X	X	X			X	X	X	X	X			X	X	X
IA		X		X			X			X		X	X	X					
MA		X	X	X	X	X	X	X		X		X	X	X			X	X	X
MI		X			X					X		k-2	X	X			X		X
NJ		X				X	Permits			X				X			X		X
TX		X		X		X	X	X				X	X	X			X	X	
WA		X		X	X			X	X	X							X		
WI		X			X	X	X	X		X		X	X				X		X
GUAM			X	X										X				X	
TOTAL	1	12	3 GUAM	7 GUAM	9	7	7	8	2	11	1	10	8	9 GUAM	1	1	10	6 GUAM	9

Source: U.S. Department of Education, National Clearinghouse for Bilingual Education. (1985) State Education Agency Information 1984-85.

TABLE C

Summary of Provisions Contained in State Legislation Permitting
Special Services for Limited-English Proficient Students

STATE	Immersion	Transitional	Maintenance	ESL	Provision of LEP Status	No Segregation	Includes Mono Lingual Speakers	Entry/Exit Criteria	Minimum Competency Testing	Student Evaluation	Annual Exam in English	Parental Consent	Parental/Community Involvement	Cultural Component	Outlines of Methodology	State Gov. Council	Avail. of State Funds	Staff Development Funds	Enforcement of Legislation	Multicultural Educ. Legislation
CO		X		X	X	X		X		X		X					X		X	
IN		X		X		X	X			X		X	X	X			X			
KS		X		X																X
ME		X	X																	
MN		X		X	X	X		X		X		X	X				X			
NH																				
NM		X	X	X	X	X	X	X		X		X	X	X			X			
NY		X		X	X	X		X	X	X		X[a]	X	X			X	X	X	
OR	X	X																		
RI		X		X	X			X		X	X						X		X	
SD																				
UT		X	X	X	X		X			X	X		X	X			X	X		
AM. SM.		X	X	X										X						
VI		X			X							X	X	X						
TOTAL	1	10 AS VI	3 AS	8 AS	6 VI	5	3	5	1	7	2	6 VI	5 VI	4 AS VI			7	2	3	1

[a]Notification required

Source: U.S. Department of Education, National Clearinghouse for Bilingual Education. (1985) State Education Agency Information 1984-85.

Seventeen states offer teacher certification in bilingual education and English as a second language, four states offer certification in bilingual education only, and seven states offer only certification in English as a second language (Table A). Some states and territories that have no state legislation mandating or permitting special education services for limited-English-proficient students require teaching credentials in bilingual education or ESL; these jurisdictions include Delaware, Washington, D.C., Florida, Hawaii, Kentucky, Louisiana, Nebraska, Nevada, North Carolina, Ohio, Tennessee, Vermont, Virginia and Puerto Rico.

THE FEDERAL CONTRIBUTION TO STATES' PROGRAMS

The federal government contributes to state bilingual education programs through Title VII grants made to states. Each state is eligible for an amount of up to 5 percent of the Title VII monies received by the local education agencies (LEAs) within the state the preceding year, and no state can receive less than $50,000 (beginning with the 1984 Bilingual Education Act). In 1986, forty-two state educational agencies (SEAs) received a total of $4,361,243 for data collection, evaluation, and technical assistance. California received the most funding ($986,973), followed by New York ($836,061), Michigan ($189,721), Texas ($170,952), Arizona ($127,107), Massachusetts ($120,079) and Florida ($115,000). Twenty-eight other states received the minimum $50,000 award.

In a survey of SEA Title VII programs conducted by SRA Technologies, Inc. (1985) before the reauthorization of the Bilingual Education Act of 1984, the following issues emerged regarding the relationship between state and federal offices of bilingual education. (a) The nature of the Title VII funding formula encouraged SEAs to help school districts write proposals for Title VII grants (states received up to 5 percent of federal funds to LEAs). (b) SEA staff members felt that submitting proposals for money for education state departments to the Office of Bilingual Education and Minority Language Affairs (OBEMLA) was unnecessary because it seemed that grants were awarded pro forma, based on the amount of federal Title VII funding to local districts the states received. (c) The services SEAs provided differed in two aspects from Title VII program regulations that defined the state role as coordinating technical assistance. First, SEA clients included all school districts that served LEP students, not just Title VII-funded districts. Second, the

SEA staff used the grant to coordinate as well as to provide technical assistance directly to LEAs; (d) SEA staff indicated they would like statutory and regulatory changes to give them more authority over funding decisions and more responsibility for monitoring local programs. (e) SEA staff wanted more frequent contact with OBEMLA, especially about Title VII awards and their conditions. (f) SEA staff wanted to know about OBEMLA monitoring visits and were interested in more extensive feedback from OBEMLA on their (SEA) performance. (g) Because Multifunctional Resource Centers had been placed under a contractual rather than a grant agreement (only allowed to carry out activities specified in the contract), they were less flexible and less useful as assistance providers. (h) States with few grants, specifically those with grants totaling less than $25,000, did not have the resources to provide technical assistance to schools with bilingual education programs.

With the passage of the 1984 Bilingual Education Act, some changes were made to address these issues. A major change was that states were given funds to carry out more activities than simply the coordination of technical assistance. These activities included collecting, aggregating, analyzing, and publishing data on the state's LEP population and the educational services available to them. SEA staff were also given funds for planning, developing, reviewing, and evaluating bilingual programs; providing or coordinating technical assistance; developing and administering instruments to assess the educational needs and competencies of LEP persons; and training of SEA and LEA staff. Funds were to supplement, not supplant, state funding.

STATE DEPARTMENT REPORTS ON TRAINING AND RESOURCE NEEDS, CAPACITY BUILDING ACTIVITIES, AND GOALS

A recent survey of state departments of education by English Language Consultants (1987) indicates the numbers of states that report a need for further training of personnel and for resources needed to develop, operate and improve services. As for further training: Twenty-one states report the need for training in methodology; thirteen states in subject areas; eight in program design and evaluation; seven in training of aides; six in materials development; and eight in identification and assessment of LEP students. As for resources needed to develop and improve programs: Forty-six states report a need for materials and thirty-one for additional staff, twenty for staff and parent training, thirteen for funds, eight for assessment and data collection, six for evaluation strategies, and five for parental involvement strategies.

States are engaged in expanding the capacity of local programs through increased training for staff (9), developing curriculum guides (8), and instructional materials (8), using state and local resources (6), increasing parental and community involvement (3), improving evaluation capability (1), and encouraging participation of non-project teachers (1).

Major state department educational goals include: improving the overall English proficiency of LEP students (22), bringing LEP students to the level of all-English classrooms (16), staff development (15), increasing parental involvement (12), improving the overall academic achievement of LEP students (10), enhancing the self-image and cultural awareness of LEP students (9), providing subject-matter content in native languages (6), and developing materials (4).

TWO CASE STUDIES

State departments of education implement state law and oversee the administration of programs for limited-English-proficient students. These two roles are described in the following case studies.

Translating Legislation into Practice: Case Study One — Arizona

One responsibility of the Office of Bilingual Education is to translate legislation into specific rules and regulations that define educational practice. In August 1984, Arizona approved comprehensive legislation related to the education of language minority students. The bill was modeled on legislation passed in California. This case study focuses on five aspects of the legislation for which policy had to be formulated.

1. Identification of language minority students;
2. Assessment of language minority students in English comprehension, speaking, reading, writing, and — for those deemed limited English proficient — a parallel assessment in the native language;
3. Selection of program options;
4. Assessment for reclassification; and
5. Development of teacher certification requirements.

In the process of establishing rules and regulations, a number of criteria were identified and used to determine the adequacy of the require-

ments under consideration: (a) availability of human and fiscal resources to implement the policy; a well-conceptualized policy that has
little potential for implementation serves no purpose. (b) Appearance
of reasonableness; it must appeal to common sense. (c) Grounding in
current practice; policy that requires little systematic realignment with
current public school practices will be easier to implement. (d) Precedents in other local, state, or federal policies; risk is minimized when a
policy-making body at the local or state level knows that others are currently engaged in the same practice. Examples of the ease of "following
suit" can be found in the career ladder/merit pay system and in competency testing. (e) Basis in descriptive or experimental research and/or
program evaluations as well as the advice of other recognized "experts,"
including staff from other SEAs, the Office for Civil Rights, universities, professional education associations, and the public schools. (f)
Fulfillment of its original intent — in this case, to protect the rights of
language minority students.

Arizona used the above criteria in formulating policy in each of the
five areas. Although not all criteria were used in all cases, to the extent
that they were approximated, the viability of the policy was enhanced.
Each of the five policy areas will be discussed with regard to these criteria.

Identification. The first task was to identify students whose first
language was not English, since this is useful in determining which students are likely to be limited English proficient. Various past procedures
to gather information on home language were reviewed. These procedures include those used in national surveys of the U.S. language
minority population. In the Language Supplement to the 1975 Current
Population Survey of the Census Bureau (U.S. Department of Commerce, 1975), data on home language use were collected by interviewing
adults for 10-15 minutes in a stratified random sample of 47,000 households. The Bureau of the Census with support from the National Center
for Educational Statistics (Waggoner, 1978) collected data in the 1978
Survey of Income and Education by conducting household interviews in
51 independent state samples of 160,000 households. The 1980 census
also used survey questions on language use, such as "Do you speak a language besides English? Well, or not at all?"

In the process of reviewing past efforts at identifying the home language use to determine an appropriate strategy for Arizona, the following procedures were assessed: (a) conducting household interviews in
which one adult provided information on language background of other
members, (b) sampling the population, rather than interviewing every-

one, (c) using self-report, (d) limiting the length of the interview to 10-15 minutes, and (e) administering a survey to all parents upon the enrollment of children in school.

Arizona decided to use option (e) and apply the LAU remedies standard for language identification set by the U.S. Department of Education between 1976 and 1981 as a way to identify students with a non-English first language. Under the LAU standards, the students primary home language is considered to be other than English if the language most often spoken in the student's home is not English, regardless of the language spoken by the student; the language most often spoken by the student is not English; or the student's first acquired language is not English.

These procedures met the criteria for adequacy for several reasons. First, many districts already collected data in this way, particularly the 25 districts under LAU compliance plans. Second, collecting data in this way was more feasible than face-to-face household interviews conducted by individuals, because all students had to enroll in school. Finally, the procedure would protect the rights of language minority students, if it were properly implemented, because they all would be interviewed.

The major concern throughout the identification phase was that the procedures could be poorly implemented. Parents, for example, might not understand the procedure because of their limited English language and literacy skills, or they might not wish to identify themselves as non-English speakers because of a fear of stigma. School staff might be untrained and unable to explain the procedure. Some districts might allow high school students to enroll themselves, or the districts might not implement these procedures because identifying potential LEP students triggers the requirement for assessment and potential provision of services. Finally, SEA staff still wondered whether the questions in the survey predicted those children most likely to be limited English proficient and whether other methods might be more appropriate.

Assessment of Language Proficiency. The second task was to determine how to assess the English language proficiency of students with a non-English home language, and what criteria to use to place them in special programs. The state adopted the following policy: Districts were permitted to screen students in grades 2-12 for achievement on a reading comprehension subtest. Students who scored above the fortieth percentile were not required to be given further assessment unless the students' parents or district staff felt that assessment was warranted. Students who scored at or below the fortieth percentile and children in kindergarten and first grade were to be given a state-approved English oral language assessment test. Students in kindergarten and first grade who scored below the publisher's designated cutoff score were considered LEP. No measures of literacy were required for children in kindergarten and first grade. For students in grades 2-12, scoring at or below the fortieth percentile, reviews of their performance on state-required criterion-referenced grade-level tests were to be conducted as well as oral assessments on state-approved instruments. Students not fluent on oral English measures and students who, although found to be proficient on these measures, were below district grade-level standards in reading or writing were considered LEP. This process identified a wide array of abilities among those classified as LEP. In addition, students not identified or assessed through these procedures could be referred by the child's parent or district staff member to receive a thorough assessment of language proficiency. LEP students were then assessed in their primary language.

In determining which students were limited English proficient, the state education department wanted to meet the criteria for sound policy. The decision to use the fortieth percentile as a screening level was based on previous research including articles by De Avila, Cervantes and Duncan (1978), Gillmore and Dickerson (1979), Gunther (1982), and Ulibarri, Spencer and Rivas (1981). The articles documented the relationship between language proficiency test scores and school achievement. Other states, including Texas and Michigan, also used this cutoff score. The fortieth percentile was reasonable since it was somewhat below average. It was current practice in districts that used the fortieth percentile as a Chapter 1 assessment procedure and as a Title VII screening procedure. There was also a very practical reason for using a standardized achievement test taken annually by all Arizona students in grades 2-12: a review of a student's cumulative file would provide the necessary information. By adapting these procedures the rights of language minority students were protected on two counts. Even though the cutoff score was arbitrary, the referral system provided a safety measure. Assessment outcomes were not contingent upon one score. Since the state administered the achievement testing program, it could ask for reports from districts of the students whose primary language was not English and who scored at or below the fortieth percentile, thus ensuring that all students whose primary language was not English would receive a thorough language assessment.

SEA staff were still concerned about the appropriateness of using a percentile ranking to predict potential LEP status. There were conflicting research findings regarding the interaction between English language proficiency, socioeconomic status, and school achievement. Rosenthal, Milne, Ginsburg, and Baker (1981) found that factors other than language background might account for most of the lower achievement of many language minority children. On the other hand, So and Chan (1984) found that language accounted for more than half of the variance in achievement. Juarez and Associates (1981) found that when socioeconomic status is controlled in Head Start programs, instructional interventions that attend to language can make a significant difference in student achievement. Determining how language minority students differed from other underachievers was problematic. Were they limited English proficient in only reading and writing, or did they lack substantive skills in other areas? Was there some other widely used measure of performance that might serve this purpose? SEA staff were concerned that districts might not inform parents and staff of their right to refer students who scored over the fortieth percentile. Also, if the referral procedures were not properly implemented, a single score above the fortieth percentile might preclude students from special services.

The SEA has to determine acceptable methods for assessing the oral language proficiency of those students who scored below the fortieth percentile on the reading comprehension subtest and for all children in kindergarten and first grade. The State Board of Education approved a number of tests for the oral English assessment including the Bilingual Syntax Measure I and II, the IDEA Oral Language Proficiency Test I and II, and the Language Assessment Scales I and II. Districts had the right to request to use a test not officially listed, but had to make the requests on an annual basis and receive state permission. Districts conducting oral language proficiency assessments before August 1984 could use the same tests for 1984-1985 if they individually assessed comprehension and speaking.

The decision to use an individual assessment and which assessment to use was based on research, other state procedures, and common sense. Teacher ratings were not selected, because research (De Avila and Duncan, 1980) and expert opinion (Gray, 1977) indicated serious questions exist about the accuracy of such ratings in determining student language proficiency. The accuracy of teacher ratings depended to some extent on the teacher's language background, familiarity with the child, and knowledge of language development. Research and other state practices indicated which tests were most reliable and valid for oral language assessment, although all instruments were acknowledged to have some limitations (Arizona Department of Education Survey of other state procedures: NIE, 1981; Ramirez, Merino, Bye and Gold, 1982; Rosansky, 1979). There was a precedent for individual language assessments, because states with a similar legislative mandate, such as California and Texas, required them. Furthermore, fifty Arizona districts already conducted individual assessments. The procedure was reasonable, in that the population to be assessed had been reduced and districts could choose one test from a number of specific tests. Most districts selected the most common assessment instruments, and the instruments selected by the state were among the most common in national use. In addition, a mechanism was put in place that allowed districts to request use of alternative tests.

There were two major concerns. One was that the recommended language assessments were not comparable, in that the instruments did not measure the same constructs of language proficiency. The other was that if the single measure used were not valid, children in kindergarten and first grade might be improperly placed.

Selection of Program Options. Having determined which students were to be served, the districts were authorized to select from among the program options provided by law: Each school district which has ten or more limited-English-proficient (LEP) pupils in any kindergarten program or grade in any school had to provide a bilingual or ESL program for the limited-English-proficient pupils. Beginning with fiscal year 1988, classes of bilingual instruction had to be taught by teachers who possess a basic or standard certificate to teach with a bilingual education endorsement. A school district has four program options, depending in part on the grade level to be served. The first was a transitional bilingual program consisting of an organized program of instruction, conducted in kindergarten programs and grades one through six, in which participating pupils received instruction in and through English and the primary home language of the pupils. A second program was a language learning program for grades 7 through 12 consisting of a structured bilingual program to promote English language proficiency and academic achievement through the use of the pupil's primary home language for instruction in the elective and non-elective content courses required for graduation. The third program option, a bilingual-bicultural program for kindergarten and grades one through twelve, consisted of a system of instruction that uses two languages (one of which is English) as means of instruction and enables pupils to achieve competency and literacy in both languages. This instruction also includes the history and culture of Arizona and the United States, as well as customs and values of the cultures associated with the languages being taught. Finally, a formal English-as-a-Second-Language program consisted of daily instruction in English language development, including listening and speaking skills, reading and writing skills, cognitive and academic skill development in English, and a plan to develop an understanding of the history and culture of the United States, as well as an understanding of customs and values of the cultures associated with the primary home language of the pupils in the program.

Each school district with nine or fewer limited-English-proficient pupils in any kindergarten program or grade in any school had to provide these limited-English-proficient pupils with either a bilingual program or English-as-a-Second-Language program as previously described or with an individual education program. An individual education program consists of a systematic, individualized program of instruction designed to ensure equal educational opportunities for the pupil by promoting English language development and by sustaining normal academic achievement through the use of the pupil's primary home language for subject-matter instruction, to the extent possible. Individual education programs do not require teachers who have the bilingual endorsement to their teaching certificate. Under the supervision of a certificated teacher, primary home instruction may be given by paraprofessionals, community teachers or pupils with proficiency in the primary home language serving as tutors.

Districts were given flexibility in program selection. As indicated earlier, some research studies indicated bilingual education programs were effective (Dulay and Burt, 1978; Troike, 1978; Rosier and Holm, 1980; Egan and Goldsmith, 1980; Michigan State Department of Education, 1982). However, other studies indicated that there was no difference between programs that used the native language and those that did not (Danoff, 1978; Baker and deKanter, 1981; Rotberg, 1982; Dutcher, 1981). Recall that legal precedent did not specify a particular remedy, only that special services had to be provided to help LEP children succeed in all English classrooms.

The state education department wanted to help districts determine which program was most likely to be effective. However, there was still considerable debate about what kind of intervention works for what kind of student, and under what circumstances. The Office of Bilingual Education also wondered if districts would make program choices based on identified needs or on expedience only.

Assessment for Reclassification. The fourth major task was to determine when pupils had developed the necessary English skills to succeed in English-only instruction and therefore could leave bilingual education programs. Using guidelines provided by the statute, the State Board of Education developed specific criteria and methods for reclassifying students. The board decided that the language reassessment criteria and procedures should be used at least once every two years with all limited-English-proficient pupils enrolled in bilingual or ESL programs to determine if the pupils had developed the English language skills necessary to succeed in English-only instruction. For a student to be reclassified, the following criteria had to be met: The teacher must observe the student's oral English proficiency and review the student's performance on the State Board of Education's minimum competency skills in the required subjects and determine that the student is performing at a level consistent with district grade level standards. At least one of the student's parents must have an opportunity to provide input into the reclassification decision. The student must achieve the publisher's designated score for fluent English proficient on an oral language proficiency assessment test selected by the district from the State Board of Education's approved list; must demonstrate writing skills at a level consistent with district standards for grade level; and must score at or above the thirty-sixth percentile of national norms on the reading comprehension subtest of the state pupil achievement testing program or in the thirty-first to the thirty-fifth percentile if a decision to reclassify has been made by a language assessment team.

Criteria for leaving the bilingual or ESL program were based on research (Archuleta and Cervantes, 1979; De Avila and Duncan, 1980; Curtis, Ligon and Weibly, 1980; Cummins, 1980, 1981; Winter, de Porcel and Nadeau, 1982; Cardoza, 1984; Cervantes, 1984) and on a review of guidelines used by New York, Texas and California (1980, 1984a & b). The adopted criteria protected the rights of language minority students, in that they prevented students from being removed from programs prematurely. The Office for Civil Rights advised the state that state-level criteria were necessary to ensure protection of the process. The guidelines were feasible, in that the only new requirement was oral language assessment. The procedure, however, was not a current practice, because LEP students had not been expected to meet a state standard for leaving the program.

Many issues were unresolved. What was the predictive validity of the criteria? The tests might place too high an expectation on students. Was it reasonable to select percentile ranking on a standardized achievement test when such tests are designed to distribute students on a normal curve? Some advocates said that when language minority students are distributed in normal fashion on such measures, the standard may be reasonable. What constitutes the "critical mass" of English language ability such that language difference no longer inhibits academic learning in English—or, to use Cummin's theory (1981), How much cognitive academic language proficiency is enough?

Certification of Teachers. Finally, the legislation required teachers in bilingual programs to hold a bilingual endorsement. The State Board of Education established a similar requirement for ESL teachers. The requirements for a bilingual endorsement are:

1. Certification in elementary, secondary, or special education.
2. Twenty-one hours of classes of which fifteen must be at the graduate level or upper division. The twenty-one hours must include classes in foundations of instruction for language minority students; methodology; linguistics; school, community, family culture, and parental involvement.
3. Student teaching in a bilingual setting or two years of successful, verifiable bilingual teaching experience.
4. Demonstrated proficiency in the non-English language to be used for instruction.

The requirements for an English-as-a-second-language endorsement include the same first two requirements of the bilingual endorsement as well as second-language learning experience and classes in the nature and grammar of the English language.

The rationale for the specific competencies for bilingual education and ESL teachers had a basis in research (Center for Applied Linguistics, 1974; Acosta and Blanco, 1978; Blachford, 1982; Binkely et al., 1981; Ramirez, 1979; Garcia and Marin, 1979; Merino and Politzer, 1977; U.S. Dept. of Education, 1984). The Michigan State Department of Education (1982) had found that student scholastic gains were highly correlated with using credentialed bilingual teachers. Other factors were also considered: there was a precedent for credentials in general, and teachers were expected to be trained and credentialed for their teaching assignments. Court cases in other states also had set a precedent. In *Castañeda v. Pickard* (1981), for example, the court stated that: "A bilingual education program, however sound in theory, is clearly unlikely to have a significant impact on language barriers confronting limited-English-speaking school children if the teachers charged with the day-to-day responsibility for the education of these children are termed qualified despite the fact that they operate under their own unremedied language ability."

The policy met the criteria of feasibility because the three state universities and many community colleges had been providing training in these fields. Some districts had required the optional bilingual credential since 1974. A phase-in period was established to make the acquisition of the credential less burdensome. The credentials would protect the rights of limited-English-proficient students by ensuring that ESL classes were not "business as usual." Credentials were supported by the Arizona Education Association. Committees of teacher trainers and practitioners advised the states to require a credential.

However, there were issues to resolve. It would be difficult to provide course work leading to a credential in rural or sparsely populated areas. There was a slight possibility that experienced bilingual or ESL teachers not having the new endorsement, and now required to have it, might leave the field. Finally, there was no assurance that the prescribed set of courses would yield a competent teacher.

Program Administration: Case Study Two—California

In states with large numbers of language minority students, the Bilingual Education Office in the State Department of Education has the major responsibility for the education of language minority students, even when these students receive support in compensatory, special, and vocational education programs, as well as in bilingual and ESL programs. California is no exception and has been selected as a case study because there are approximately 1.182 million language minority students in the state; 613,224 of them are limited English proficient. The state's Bilingual Education Office (BEO) is responsible for coordinating the administration of state and federal programs for LEP students. Funds for the BEO come from different sources, including federal Title VII grants ($22.8 million), the Emergency Immigrant Education Act ($13.9 million), the Transition Program for Refugee Children ($4.5 million), Title VI of the Civil Rights Act ($200,000), and the state ($409,739).

The Bilingual Education Office is located in the Categorial Support Programs Division of the State Department of Education, which also includes the Offices of Compensatory Education, American Indian Education, and Migrant Education. The division is located in the Curriculum and Instructional Leadership Branch, one of seven major branches that make up the Department of Education.

The BEO, which employs 14 professionals as well as clerical and support staff, is divided into three areas: administration, consultation to the field, and budget and governmental program analysis. The administrators are responsible for management of the Bilingual Education Office, fiscal planning, and for policy analysis necessary for decision making and long-range planning. The consultants provide technical assistance to local education agencies and institutes of higher learning. They coordinate services with agencies working with LEP students, including the county coordinators, the Multifunctional Support Center staff, and the National Origin Desegregation (LAU) Assistance Centers. They also gather and analyze data and distribute this information to local educational agencies and the U.S. Department of Education. Budget and program analysts develop and manage budgets which support various activities in the unit.

The BEO defines its overall role as collecting, aggregating, analyzing, and publishing data and information on LEP persons in the state and the educational services provided them. The BEO also conducts activities designed to improve the effectiveness of bilingual education programs and other services including the following:

1. **Planning and developing educational programs.** Programs that have been developed include ESEA Title VII programs, bilingual immersion programs, and programs located in schools interested in using sound research to serve limited-English-proficient students.
2. **Providing, coordinating, or supervising technical assistance and other forms of non-financial assistance to local educational agencies.** Activities include preparation and field-testing of parent education materials, meeting with county bilingual coordinators, visiting Title VII programs, and making conference presentations on topics related to language minority students.
3. **Developing and administering assessment instruments and procedures.** BEO staff participate in a technical review of language assessment instruments for possible use in the census of LEP students.
4. **Training SEA and LEA Staff.** Activities include providing a management institute for all first-year Title VII directors and for training SEA staff in their areas of professional expertise.

A recent focus of the BEO is to identify schools that are interested in serving limited-English-proficient students and then provide them with intensive technical assistance. BEO staff report that these tasks result in higher quality program implementation. They are able to demonstrate that the research on effective practice for language minority students works. Presentations by staff from the model programs attest to the validity of the research.

Less intensive assistance is provided by BEO staff through a network made up of bilingual directors from large school districts, directors of federally funded resource centers, and eighteen county-level bilingual education coordinators. The coordinators provide information to districts that together serve 90 percent of the LEP population. BEO staff meet with the coordinators and directors four times a year to disseminate information and use them as a sounding board for ideas. At these meetings BEO staff provide state and federal legislative updates (for example, explaining the grant application cycle) and also substantive information about new research and program models relevant to educating LEP students. The county office staff and directors then use this information to set up staff development sessions that last a day or two, or even as long as twelve days. The coordinator network and directors help BEO decide what information is relevant and also help translate the research on effective practice into materials useful for staff development.

BEO staff have also produced several excellent books on the education of language minority students, including *Schooling and Language-Minority Students: A Theoretical Framework, Studies on Immersion Education: A Collection for United States Educators*, and *Beyond Language: Social and Cultural Factors in Schooling Language Minority Students.* The staff asks scholars to contribute chapters. They have also published handbooks for teaching Cantonese-speaking, Korean-speaking, Japanese-speaking, Filipino-speaking, Portuguese-speaking, and Vietnamese-speaking students; resource guides for bilingual-cross-cultural teacher aides and bilingual education advisory committees; and various handbooks for language minority parents and school personnel.

BEO staff work has changed significantly in the past five years. Originally, the office spent a considerable amount of time monitoring districts to assure that state and federal laws related to the education of LEP students were carried out. As school districts became familiar with the laws and honored them, BEO staff spent less time monitoring to ensure compliance and more time providing technical assistance. Since the sunset of the Bilingual Education Improvement and Reform Act in 1987 (AB 507), their focus has changed again. Because school districts now have considerable flexibility in designing educational programs for LEP students, BEO staff help districts tailor their services to the socioeducational context of the district. Although districts are no longer legally required to provide the program options defined in AB 507 (i.e. basic bilingual education, bilingual-bicultural education, individual learning programs, etc.), these options can be used as a general framework from which to develop programs.

Chapter 7

A LOOK FORWARD

THE MAJOR issue related to the education of language minority children pertains to the large number of such children failing in school. This concluding chapter will briefly describe the current situation and make suggestions about how research and policy might address the needs of these children, specifically by ensuring that all eligible children are served and that the services provided are of high quality.

CURRENT SERVICES AND RECENT TRENDS

Very few federal and state programs require native language use. The two major federal programs tailored to meet the special language needs of language minority children are the Bilingual Education Act (20 USC 3221 *et seq.*) and the Bilingual Vocational Training Program authorized by the Vocation Education Act (20 USC 2411). In 1984-85 twelve states required native language use under some circumstances. Most of the remaining states permitted native language use but did not mandate it.

Many more language minority children are served in federal and state programs that do not require native language use. Limited English proficient students participate in federal programs not restricted to them such as Chapter 1 of the Education Consolidation and Improvement Act (20 USC 3801 *et seq.*), the Vocational Education Act (20 USC *et seq.*) and the Higher Education Act (20 USC 1070 d). In fact, many more LEP students participate in the latter programs than in Title VII. Some, but not all, states have programs that specifically serve language minority children. States that have no programs assume it is the local educational agency's responsibility to provide appropriate services.

t so few programs require native language use is indicative of a
ment trend on the part of both the federal government and states which
allows local districts flexibility in deciding whether or not to use the native language. Both the 1984 and current Title VII reauthorization
(1988) provide funds for programs that use only English. Many states
also allow this flexibility. Instructive is Arizona's recent (1984) comprehensive language minority education policy as set forth in State Department of Education regulations R7-2-306. Like other comprehensive
state policies, it places specific programmatic requirements on school
districts such as serving all eligible children; however, it allows school
district flexibility in determining the actual instructional character of the
adopted programs. Therefore, all school districts with 10 or more identified language minority students per school site are mandated to provide
special language minority education programming. However, the school
district can choose from one of four (or some combination of these) program options for actual implementation.

This concept of flexibility has been adopted in other states (Gray,
1986). In 1981, Colorado passed the English Language Proficiency Act
which replaced the Colorado Education Act. This new legislation significantly increased the local option which permits flexibility in the education method for serving language minority students. Many school districts have dismantled their bilingual programs since the passage of this
law. In 1982, Rhode Island passed legislation similar to Colorado's. A
Virginia bill, adopted in 1981, declared English the official language
and stipulated that "school boards shall have no obligation to teach the
standard curriculum in a language other than English."

In addition to specific legislation which increases the flexibility local
districts have in implementing programs, there is a movement to make
English the official national or state language. (English Plus Information
Clearing House, 1988) Measures at the federal level have been introduced to advance this objective. Two versions of the English Language
Amendment (ELA) and one non-binding "sense of the Congress" resolution proclaiming English the official language of the United States are
pending in the One Hundredth Congress. The first version of the ELA is
embodied in Senate Joint Resolution 13, House Joint Resolution 33, and
House Joint Resolution 83 and states: "(1) The English language shall
be the official language of the United States. (2) The Congress shall
have the power to enforce this article by the appropriate legislation." The
second version embodied in H.J. Res. 13 and H.J. Res. 60 contains two
additional provisions: "(1) Neither the United States nor any state shall

require by law, ordinance, regulation, order, decree, program, or policy, the use in the United States of any language other than English. (2) This article shall not prohibit any law, ordinance, regulation, order, decree, program, or policy requiring educational instruction in a language other than English for the purpose of making students who use a language other than English proficient in English."

In 1986, California passed proposition 63 which amends the state constitution to prevent the legislature from passing any law which diminishes or ignores the role of English as a common language. There are twelve other states with official English laws, including Arkansas, Mississippi, North Dakota, Georgia, Virginia, Indiana, Kentucky, Tennessee, Illinois, North Carolina, South Carolina, and Nebraska. Except for Illinois, Nebraska, and Virginia, the legislation has been passed since 1984. According to the *Hispanic Link Newsletter* (1987) only two official English states have Hispanic populations over 100,000 and they include California and Illinois. Attempts to pass official English legislation in three other states with large Hispanic populations (i.e. Arizona, Colorado and New Mexico) have been unsuccessful. Three state constitutions protect the use of other languages: Hawaii, Louisiana, and New Mexico.

ACADEMIC ACHIEVEMENT OF LANGUAGE MINORITY STUDENTS

Based on reading tests given in 1983 and 1984, the National Assessment of Educational Progress (1986) reported that, on the average, language minority students, especially Hispanic students, were considerably below the national average at grades 4, 8, and 11. Furthermore, they were likely to be older than the typical student, less likely to have taken advanced science and math classes, and more likely to expect that they will not graduate from high school. Although not all language minority students are limited English proficient now (according to the National Assessment of Educational Progress definition), many may have been in their early years. We also know that individuals from non-English language backgrounds drop out at four times the rate if they themselves do not speak English (Steinberg, Blinde and Chan, 1984).

School failure may result in part from the low enrollment of limited-English-proficient students in bilingual or ESL classes. Data from the National Assessment of Education Progress (1986) indicate that among Hispanics with limited proficiency in English, less than 45 percent were in programs specifically designed to address the language difference. Among the non-Hispanic language minority children less than 25 percent were in such classes.

That so many children are unserved is unsettling, since both a Supreme Court decision and federal law require that these children be served. The U.S. Supreme Court, in the 1974 *Lau v. Nichols* decision, ordered school districts receiving federal funds to take affirmative steps to overcome the English language deficiencies of students with limited English-speaking ability. The 1974 Equal Educational Opportunities and Transportation of Students Act (29 USC 1701 *et seq.*) and related regulations require that education agencies must take appropriate action to overcome language barriers that impede equal participation by students in instructional programs.

Lack of enforcement of the *Lau* decision and Equal Educational Opportunities Act contribute to poor service provision. One role of the Office of Civil Rights is to monitor local districts to ensure that limited-English-proficient students are provided with the services due them. Such monitoring can greatly assist in identifying and motivating service provision. However, a recent report on compliance by the Education Department's Office for Civil Rights (OCR), reported in *Education Week* (June 4, 1986), indicates that from 1981 to 1985 school districts were nine times less likely to be scheduled for a compliance review than during the previous five years. Two other types of oversight—complaint investigations and monitoring visits—declined also. Under the current administration, only 20 percent of the consent agreements negotiated between OCR and school districts prior to 1981 were subjected to federal scrutiny, and of the 202 enforcement actions since 1981, OCR investigators found a 58 percent rate of non-compliance. Although violators agreed to take corrective actions, OCR officials rarely returned to ensure compliance.

A current issue is whether federal legislation in coordination with state legislation and policy should establish an entitlement program whereby all eligible students are served. Such a program might parallel the Education for all Handicapped Children Act, Public Law 94-142 (20 USC 1400 *et seq.*). Before the law's enactment in 1975, virtually every state in the union excluded many children from school or put children in programs ill-suited to their needs. Public Law 94-142 ensures that every handicapped child, between the ages of three and twenty-one who resides in a state participating in the program, has a right to a free, appropriate public education in the least-restrictive environment. Currently, the federal government contributes about 10 percent of the cost of these programs and the states pay for the rest. Since methods to identify language minority students in need of special services are available and used in numerous states, this might be a feasible approach to guaranteeing services to all needy language minority children.

It is clear that more children need services, but debate continues about why such large numbers of language minority students fail and the best methods to educate them. Critics of programs that require native language use contend that students' failure is a consequence of such programs since they prevent students from acquiring English. Education Secretary William Bennett (1985) described the present federal policy, with its emphasis on instruction in the student's native language, as "confused" and "overbearing" and called for local flexibility in program design to help students acquire English as quickly as possible. On the other hand, numerous policymakers, educators, and advocates maintain that research supports native language programming as a valid methodology.

IMPROVING PROGRAM QUALITY

Research

Because of the failure of so many children, it is clear that both evaluation research and basic research are needed to inform policymakers and educators so that high-quality programs are put in place. Because policymakers require information about the overall effectiveness of federal or state efforts, large-scale evaluations are necessary. For this purpose, meta-analysis appears more promising than narrative reviews. However, meta-analysis has its limitations, since it is based on primary studies in which equating treatment and comparison groups with statistical procedure is difficult, and random assignment is usually not possible. As an alternative, Willig (1985) recommends that research centers, collaborating with school districts willing to participate, implement well-designed experimental models rather than program/no-program comparisons. With the knowledge gained from these studies, schools could incorporate aspects of a model conducive to their own student population and objectives.

Basic research must continue to elucidate how children best acquire a second language in instructional settings. Current research has focused on the importance of culturally sensitive teaching strategies and classroom organization and on the use of native languages. Recent findings demonstrate that cognitive, cultural background, and social variables influence knowledge acquisition in general and second-language acquisition in particular (Phillips, 1983, 1984; McLaughlin, 1985; Wong-Fillmore et al., 1985; Garcia, 1986). Further research on how best to organize instructional settings and construct curriculum for culturally different children is critically important.

Recent findings also highlight the importance of using students' first language. Tikenoff (1983) and Wong-Fillmore and colleagues (1985) report that children in classes where first language was used appeared to be more involved in learning and to participate more actively in classroom discussions. Cummins (1984) and Hakuta (1986) maintain that skills learned in one language transfer to another, and that a conceptual framework in the native language provides "scaffolding" for the acquisition of new knowledge in the second language. Children at risk of failing in school especially need language, literacy, and conceptual development in their first language. However, more research is needed to ascertain the benefits of classroom use of native language in the cognitive, social, and emotional development of language minority students.

Research informed by the experience and needs of practitioners and policymakers is more relevant and more likely to be useful in improving educational conditions for language minority children. A promising new approach to research involves collaboration between researchers and practitioners as well as between researchers and policymakers. With this in mind, the University of California initiated the Linguistic Minority Project. Its formation was a result of concern about the failure of elementary and secondary language minority students, defined as students whose first language is not English, those who speak a minority dialect of English, and those whose physical handicap interferes with linguistic performance. Researchers work with practitioners and policymakers to develop a research agenda that will explore the causes of students' school failure and attempt solutions. Research results are widely disseminated to researchers, practitioners, policymakers.

The Inter-University Program for Latino Research (IUP) was established by four universities with strong centers for research on Hispanics at the Stanford Center for Chicano Research, the Chicano Studies Research Center at the University of California at Los Angeles, the Center for Mexican American Studies at the University of Texas at Austin, and the Centro de Estudios Puertoriqueños at Hunter College of the City University of New York. The object of the program is to encourage systematic communication and cooperation among the centers and the development of joint research projects. Among these projects are those that include language and education. One goal of the project is to provide research-based information to policymakers. Linkage activities between IUP and the California legislature are currently underway.

The Hispanic Policy Development Project, located in Washington, D.C. and New York City, is a private organization that conducts research on Hispanics. It is currently sponsoring a small grants competition to promote collaboration between researchers and legislators, education practitioners, or policymakers with the goal of improving the retention rate and raising achievement levels of at-risk Hispanic junior and senior high school students.

Litigation

Research is one way to improve program quality. Litigation is another. Holding districts accountable for the performance of limited-English-proficient children is one strategy used by the courts to improve program quality. The 1974 Equal Educational Opportunity Act (EEOP) reaffirmed by the *Castañeda* and *Keyes* decisions set out standards that all states have an obligation to follow. The courts in the *Castañeda v. Pickard* (1981) decision set a precedent in this area. The decision stated that:

1. The language minority education program must be based on a sound educational theory;
2. The program must be reasonably calculated to implement effectively (with staff and other resources) the chosen theory; and
3. The program must produce identifiable results in a reasonable time.

As a consequence of the above guidelines, a landmark remedial plan was negotiated out of court in Denver, Colorado (*Keyes v. School District No. 1, Denver*). As did *Castañeda*, it entailed developing a sound program, establishing a method to determine if the program was working, and revisions to improve components that weren't working. Two other decisions based on the 1974 EEOP and *Keyes* and *Castañeda* reaffirm a state's responsibility to make sure appropriate standards are followed. In *Idaho Migrant Council v. Board of Education* (647 F 269 9th cir., 1981), it was determined that the state had an obligation to monitor compliance by local education associations and based on *Gomez v. Illinois State Board of Education* (811 F2 1030 7th cir., 1987) the state has an obligation to set and monitor minimal standards.

State and Federal Policies

States and the federal government have used a variety of strategies to improve program quality. Some states and the federal government have required certain program provisions to be incorporated into programs serving language minority children. Such provisions may include, for example, entry and exit criteria, parental involvement, teacher certification, student assessment, program evaluation, etc. They have generally provided additional aid so that these requirements can be implemented. Technical assistance has been used to improve program quality. Title VII provides funds to states so that they can provide technical assistance to local districts. Title VII also provides mechanisms for technical assistance through the network of multifunctional resource centers and the evaluation assistance centers. States have their own mechanisms for technical assistance which include information dissemination through newsletters, books, and meetings as well as site visits. Another way they promote quality is by identifying highly successful programs and promoting these as models to other constituent districts. California has begun such a project by selecting districts highly motivated to implement the state law, working comprehensively with those districts and developing case studies. Such case studies allow the testing of a specific theoretical framework for educating language minority students, allow inspection of program staffing, resources and instructional attributes, and permit a thorough examination of program results.

Systematic improvement is generally difficult to implement, since few states have comprehensive data that indicate how well limited English proficient children are served. One state can be used to exemplify this and to point to some possible solutions. A recent report by this state's Bureau of Equal Educational Opportunity, *Seeking Educational Equity for Linguistic Minority Students,* expresses concern about the large numbers of limited-English-proficient students who are failing in school, especially Hispanic students. School failure is "deduced from the high dropout rates," but the data neither illuminates why this is so nor indicates which language minorities are at risk. For example, under the Board of Education's Basic Skills Improvement Policy, an annual assessment is made of the number and proportion of students who meet minimum standards in the basic skills. School systems determine what evaluation instruments will be used, set a minimum standard, and may exempt certain students from the assessment program. As a result of this local flexibility, many Hispanic students were exempted from testing in

1984-85 (the proportion of Hispanics exempted from reading in grades K-3 was 38%; grades 4-6, 36%; grades 7-12, 35%). As a result, there is no accurate statewide information about the educational status of these children. For Hispanic students who were included in the testing program, a large proportion failed to meet even minimum competencies; in grades K-3, 16% in reading, 12% in math; in grades 4-6, 22% in reading and 20% in math; in grades 7-12, 26% in reading, 24% in math. As indicated by the data, Hispanic students do progressively worse as they progress through the system (if it can be assumed that children in the later grades were in the system in the early grades).

Other students, mostly Asian, also obtain lower scores in reading at the secondary level: whereas in the early elementary grades 4 percent do not meet minimum standards, by the secondary grades 16 percent do not meet these standards. As with the Hispanic samples, it is unclear how long the children in secondary schools have been in the school system. Nor does the data describe the educational experience these students have had, including type and quality of programs.

In order to find out what relationship exists between educational programs and academic achievement, the board prepared a special report on Asian and Hispanic students who entered the system in 1980-81. In 1985-86, 19 percent of Asian students and 68 percent of Hispanic students were still in bilingual education programs. However, no data is presented to indicate how these students were doing or how they might compare with similar students who exited earlier.

The method least used by states to improve program quality is to establish performance outcomes for local districts and to monitor and intervene with technical assistance, or even managerial takeover, when the outcomes are not satisfactory. As previously mentioned, court cases have established a precedent for this policy, but it is not generally practiced without litigation. Given the number of limited-English-proficient children failing in school and the legal precedent for this policy, this alternative may need to receive more serious consideration in the future.

CONCLUSION

Large numbers of language minority children continue to fail in school, and the number of such children will increase given present demographic trends. Data from the 1980 census indicate that 4.5 million school-age children speak a language other than English at home, nearly

10 percent of all U.S. children in the public school-age range; and this sector is the fastest-growing segment of the U.S. population. By the year 2000, the number of language minority children is expected to increase by more than 35 percent in the 5-14 age range.

Our limited-English-proficient children are a human resource. A sound education is important not only for their own eventual economic well-being but for the well-being of our society as a whole, politically and socially as well as economically. By the year 2000 one of five workers will be a member of a language minority group. Our nation needs competent, skilled workers in order to compete in the world marketplace. Moreover, our society is aging rapidly and thus is increasingly dependent on high productivity from future generations to meet its economic needs and shoulder public responsibilities. Between 1980 and 2020 the number of workers contributing to the Social Security system for each Social Security recipient will drop by nearly one-third. And by the 1990s one of three workers will be a member of a minority group.

Language minority children must receive the educational services necessary to help them overcome educational barriers. Research must continue to inform national, state, and local policy and practice; court decisions must ensure that all children are served well; and state and federal policy must guarantee that educational institutions respond to this constituency's particular needs.

BIBLIOGRAPHY

Acosta, R., and Blanco, F. (1978). *Competencies for University Programs in Bilingual Education*. Washington, D.C.: U.S. Government Printing Office.

Anderson, T., and Boyer, M. (1970). *Bilingual Schooling in the United States*. Austin, TX: Southwest Educational Laboratory.

Archuleta, K., and Cervantes, R. (1979). *Bilingual Reclassification Criteria Report*. Sacramento, CA: California Department of Education.

Beardsmore, H.B. (1982). *Bilingualism: Basic Principles*. Clevedon, England: Multilingual Matters.

Baker, K.A. and deKanter, A.A. (1983, July). An Answer From Research on Bilingual Education. *American Education*, 48-88.

Baker, K.A., and deKanter, A.A. (1981, September). *Effectiveness of Bilingual Education: A Review of the Literature*. Washington, D.C.: Office of Planning, Budget and Evaluation, U.S. Department of Education.

Baratz, J., and Duran, R. (1986). *The Educational Progress of Language-Minority Students: Findings From the 1983-84 NAEP Reading Survey*. Princeton, N.J.: National Assessment of Education Progress (NAEP CN-6710).

Barik, H.C., and Swain, M. (1975). Three Year Evaluation of a Large Scale Early Grade French Immersion Program: The Ottawa Study. *Language Learning*, 25, 1-30.

Bates, E. (1976). *Language in Context: The Acquisition of Pragmatics*. New York, Academic Press.

Ben-Zeev, S. (1977). The Influence of Bilingualism on Cognitive Strategy and Cognitive Development. *Child Development*, 48, 1009-1018.

Ben-Zeev, S. (1977). The Effect of Spanish-English Bilingualism in Children From Less Privileged Neighborhoods on Cognitive Development and Cognitive Strategy. *Working Papers on Bilingualism*, 14, 83-122.

Binkely, J., Johnson, D., Stewart, B., Abrica-Carrasco, R., Nava, H., and Thrope, B. (1981). *A Study of Teacher Training Programs in Bilingual Education. Vol. I: Program Descriptions*. RMC Report No. UR-474. Mountain View, CA: RMC Research Corporation.

Birman, Beatrice F., and Ginsburg, Alan L. (1981). Addressing the Needs of Language-Minority Children: Issues of Federal Policy. U.S. Department of Education, Office of Planning, Budget, and Evaluation.

Blachford, C.H. (1982). *Directory of Teacher Preparation Programs in TESOL and Bilingual Education: 1981-1984*. Washington, D.C.: Teachers of English to Speakers of Other Languages.

Bloom, L. (1978). *Readings in Language Development*. New York: John Wiley and Sons.

Boggs, S. (1972). The Meaning of Questions and Narratives to Hawaiian Children. In C. Cazden, V. John, and D. Hymes (Eds.), *Functions of Language in the Classroom*. New York: Teachers College Press.

Bowerman, M. (1973). Crosslinguistic Similarities at Two Stages of Syntactic Development. In E. Lenneberg and E. Lenneberg, *Foundations of Language Development*. London: UNESCO Press.

Braine, M.D.S. (1976). Children's First Word Combination. *Monographs of the Society for Research in Child Development*. New York: John Wiley and Sons.

Brooks, R. (1966). The Jurisprudence of Willard Hurst. *Journal of Legal Education*, 18, 257-264.

Brown, R. (1983). Development of the First Language in the Human Species. *American Psychologist*, 28, 97-106.

Brown vs. Board of Education. 347 US 483, 1954; 686.

California State Department of Education. (1986). *Beyond Language: Social and Cultural Factors in Schooling Language-Minority Students*. Los Angeles, California: Evaluation, Dissemination and Assessment Center, California State University, Los Angeles.

California State Department of Education. (1984, November). *Legal Requirements for the Implementation of State Bilingual Programs*. Sacramento, CA: California Department of Education.

California State Department of Education. (1984, June). *SB 813: Review of Language Reclassification — An Advisory Committee Report to Superintendent Honig and the State Board of Education*. Sacramento, CA: California Department of Education.

California State Department of Education. (1984). *Studies on Immersion Education: A Collection for United States Educators*. Los Angeles, CA: Evaluation, Dissemination and Assessment Center, California State University, Los Angeles.

California State Department of Education. (1981). *Schooling and Language-Minority Students: A Theoretical Framework*. Los Angeles, CA: Evaluation, Dissemination and Assessment Center, California State University, Los Angeles.

California State Department of Education. (1980, November). *Interim Guidelines for Language Reclassification*. Sacramento, CA: Office of Bilingual Bicultural Education.

Canale, M. (1983). From Communicative Competence to Communicative Language Pedagogy. In J. Richards and R. Schmidt (Eds.), *Language and Communication*. London: Langman.

Cardenas, J.A. (1977). An IDRA Response with Summary: The AIR Evaluation of the Impact of ESEA Title VII Spanish/English Bilingual Education Programs. San Antonio, TX: Intercultural Development Research Associates.

Cardoza, D. (1984, May). *The Reclassification Survey: A Study of Entry and Exit Classification Procedures*. Los Angeles, CA: National Center for Bilingual Research.

Carringer, D.C. (1974). Creative Thinking Abilities of Mexican Youth: The Relationship of Bilingualism. *Journal of Cross-Cultural Psychology*, 5, 492-504.

Castañeda vs. Pickard, 648 F.2d 989, 1007 5th Cir. 1981; 103 S. Ct. 3321 (1983).

Cazden, C. (1972). *Child Language and Education*. New York: Holt, Rinehart and Winston.

Center for Applied Linguistics (CAL). (1974). *Guidelines for the Preparation and Certification of Teachers of Bilingual/Bicultural Education.* Arlington, VA: Center for Applied Linguistics.

Cervantes, R. (1984). *Entry Into and Exit from Bilingual Programs.* Unpublished manuscript.

Chomsky, N. (1959). Review of B.F. Skinner, *Verbal Behavior and Language,* 35, 116-128.

Cole, M., Dore, J., Hall, W., and Dowley, G. (1978). Situation and Task in Childrens' Talk. *Discourse Process,* 1, 119-126.

Commission on Reading. (1986). *Becoming a Nation of Readers.* Washington, D.C.: U.S. Department of Education, National Institutes of Education.

Congressional Research Service (CRS). (1984). *Bilingual Education: Federal Policy Issue.* Report No. IB-83131, July 6.

Corder, S.P. (1967). The Significance of Learner's Errors. *International Review of Applied Linguistics in Language Teaching,* 14, 138-156.

Crawford, J. U.S. Enforcement of Bilingual Plans Declines Sharply. *Education Week,* June 4, 1986, pp. 1; 14-15. (Vol. 5, No. 37).

Cummins, J. (1984). *Bilingualism and Special Education.* San Diego: College Hill Press.

Cummins, J., and Gulatson, M. (1974). Some Effects of Bilingualism in Cognitive Functioning. In T. Carey (Ed.), *Bilingualism, Biculturalism and Education.* Alberta, Canada: University of Alberta, Edmonton, 129-137.

Cummins, J. (1979). Linguistic Interdependence and the Educational Development of Bilingual Children. *Review of Educational Research,* 19, 222-251.

Cummins, J. (1980). The Entry and Exit Fallacy in Bilingual Education. *NABE Journal, Vol. IV,* (3) p. 25-60.

Cummins, J. (1981). The Role of Primary Language Development in Promoting Educational Success for Language Minority Students. In California State Department of Education (Ed.), *Schooling and Language Minority Students: A Theoretical Framework.* Los Angeles, CA: Evaluation, Dissemination and Assessment Center, California State University, Los Angeles, 3-49.

Curtis, J., Ligon, G., and Weibley, G. (1980). When is a LEP No Longer a LEP? *Bilingual Education Paper Series.* Vol. 3. No. 8. Los Angeles, CA: National Dissemination and Assessment Center. California State University.

Cziko, G.A. (1978). Differences in First and Second-Language Reading: The Use of Syntactic, Semantic and Discourse Constraints. *Canadian Modern Language Review,* 34, 473-489.

Danoff, M.N. (1978). *Evaluation of the Impact of ESEA Title VII Spanish/English Bilingual Education Program: Overview of Study and Findings.* Palo Alto, CA: American Institutes for Research.

Darcy, N.T. (1953). A Review of the Literature of the Effects of Bilingualism Upon the Measurement of Intelligence. *Journal of Genetic Psychology,* 82, 21-57.

Darcy, N.T. (1963). Bilingualism and the Measurement of Intelligence: Review of a Decade of Research. *Journal of Genetic Psychology,* 103, 259-282.

DeAvila, E.A., Duncan, S.E., Ulibarri, D.M., and Fleming, J.S. (1983). Predicting the Academic Success of Language Minority Students from Developmental, Cognitive Style, Linguistic and Teacher Perception Measures. In E. Garcia (Ed.), *The Mexican American Child.* Tempe, AZ: Arizona State University, 50-66.

DeAvila, E.A., and Duncan, S.E. (1980). Definition and Measurement of Bilingual Students. In R. Cervantes (Ed.), *Bilingual Program, Policy, and Assessment Issues*. Sacramento, CA: California Department of Education.

DeAvila, E.A., Cervantes, R.A., and Duncan, S.E. (1978). Bilingual Program Criteria. Report submitted to the Office of Program Evaluation and Research, California Department of Education.

Department of Health, Education and Welfare. (1970). May 25, 1970 Memorandum. *Federal Register*, 35, 11595.

Development Associates. (1984, December). Final Report Descriptive Study Phase of the National Longitudinal Evaluation of the Effectiveness of Services for Language Minority Limited English Proficient Students. Arlington, VA: Development Associates.

deVillier, J., and deVillier, P. (1978). *Language Acquisition*. Cambridge, MA: Harvard University Press.

Diaz, R.M. (1983). The Impact of Bilingualism on Cognitive Development. In E.W. Gordon (Ed.), *Review of Research in Education (Vol. X)*. Washington, D.C.: American Educational Research Association, 23-54.

Dulay, H., and Burt, M. (1978). *Why Bilingual Education? A Summary of Research Findings*. San Francisco, CA: Bloomsbury West, Inc.

Dulay, H., and Burt, M. (1974a). Errors and Strategies in Child Second Language Acquisition. *TESOL Quarterly*, 8, 2, 63-87.

Dulay, H., and Burt, M. (1974b). Natural Sequence in Child Second Language Acquisition. *Working Papers on Bilingualism*. Toronto: The Ontario Institute for Studies in Education.

Duran, R. (Ed.). (1981). *Latino Language and Communicative Behavior*. Norwood, NJ: Ablex Publishing Corporation.

Dutcher, N. (1981). *The Use of First and Second Languages in Primary Education: Selected Case Studies*. Draft Report Prepared for the Education Department of the World Bank., as cited in Rotberg, 1982.

Egan, L., and Goldsmith, R. (1980). *Bilingual-Bicultural Education: The Colorado Success Story*. Mimeographed.

Elizardo de Weffer, R.D.C. (1972). *Effects of First Language Instruction in Academic and Psychological Development of Bilingual Children*. Unpublished Ph.D. dissertation, Illinois Institute of Technology.

Engle, P.L. (1975). The Use of Vernacular Languages in Education. *Bilingual Education Series, No. 3*. Arlington, VA: Center for Applied Linguistics.

English Language Consultants. (1987). *A Summary of State Reports on a Limited-English Proficient Student Population*. Washington, D.C.: Report submitted to the United States Department of Education, Office of Bilingual Education and Language Minority Affairs.

English Plus Information Clearinghouse. (1988). *The English Language Amendment in the 100th Congress*. Mimeograph report. Washington, D.C.: The National Immigration, Refugee and Citizenship Forum.

Equal Educational Opportunities and Transportation of Students Act, 1974, 42 U.P.S.C.A. 6705.

Ervin-Tripp, S., and Mitchell-Kernan, C. (1977). *Child Discourse*. New York: Academic Press.

Ervin-Tripp, S.M. (1974). Is Second Language Learning Like the First? *TESOL Quarterly*, 8, 2, 111-127.

Feldman, C., and Shen, M. (1971). Some Language Related Cognitive Advantages of Bilingual Five-Year-Olds. *Journal of Genetic Psychology*, 118-235.

Fishman, J.A., and Lovas, S.J. (1970). Bilingual Education in a Sociolinguistic Perspective. *TESOL Quarterly*, 4, 3, 215-222.

Garcia, A.B., and Marin, E. (1979). The Relationship Between Student Language Growth and Teacher Certification in Bilingual Crosscultural Education. In Raymond V. Padilla (Ed.), *Ethnoperspectives in Bilingual Education Research, Vol. I*. Ypsilanti, MI: Department of Foreign Languages and Bilingual Studies, Eastern Michigan University, 367-375.

Garcia, E. (1983). *Bilingualism in Early Childhood*. Albuquerque, NM: University of New Mexico Press.

Garcia, E. (1986). Bilingual Development and the Education of Bilingual Children During Early Childhood. *American Journal of Education*, 95, No. 1, 96-121.

Garcia, E., and Carrasco, R. (1981). An Analysis of Bilingual Mother-Child Discourse. In R. Duran (Ed.), *Latino Discourse*. New York: Ablex Publications, 173-189.

Garcia, E., and Flores, B. (1986). *Language and Literacy Research in Bilingual Education*. Tempe, AZ: Arizona State University.

Garcia, E., and Gonzales, G. (1984). Spanish and Spanish-English Development in the Hispanic Child. In S.V. Martinez and R.H. Mendoza (Eds.), *Chicano Psychology*. New York: Academic Press.

Garcia, E., Maez, L., and Gonzalez, G. (1983). Language Switching in Bilingual Children: A National Perspective. In E. Garcia (Ed.), *The Mexican-American Child: Language Cognition and Social Development*. Tempe, AZ: Arizona State University, 56-73.

Garcia, E., Carrasco, R., and Flores, B. (1983). Transition in the Bilingual Classroom: The Bilingual Broker. American Educational Research Association, Montreal.

Garcia, E., Carrasco, R., and Flores, B. (1983). Language Functions in Bilingual Academic and Non-Academic Contexts. Paper delivered at American Educational Research Association, Montreal.

Gardner, R.C., and Lambert, E. (1972). *Attitudes and Motivation in Second Language Learning*. Rowley, MA: Newbury House.

Geissler, H. (1981). Zweisprachigkeit Deutscher Kinder im Ausland. Stuttgart: Kohlhammas.

Gillmore, G., and Dickerson, A. (1979). *The Relationship Between Instruments Used for Identifying Children of Limited English Speaking Ability in Texas*. Houston, TX: Region IV Education Service Center (ED 191 907).

Ginishi, C. (1981). Code Switching in Chicano Six Year Olds. In R. Duran (Ed.), *Latino Language and Communicative Behavior*. Norwood, NJ: Ablex Publishing Corporation, 133-152.

Gonzales, G. (1970). *The Acquisition of Spanish Grammar by Native Spanish Speakers*. Doctoral Dissertation, University of Texas at Austin, 1970.

Goodman, G. (1984, September). Significant Bilingual Instructional Features Study. San Francisco, CA: Far West Laboratory.

Goodman, K., Goodman, Y., and Flores, B. (1979). *Reading in the Bilingual Classroom: Literacy and Biliteracy.* Roslyn, VA: National Clearinghouse for Bilingual Education.

Gray, T. (1986). Language Policy and Educational Strategies for Language Minority and Majority Students in the United States. In Lorne La Forge (Ed.), *Proceedings of the International Colloquium on Language Planning.* Paris: Les Presses de L'University Laval.

Gray, T. (1977). *Response to the AIR study "Evaluation of the Impact of ESEA Title VII Spanish/English Bilingual Education Program."* Arlington, VA: Center for Applied Linguistics. Arlington, VA.

Guadalupe vs. Tempe Elementary School District No. 3, 587 F.2d 1022 (9th Cir. 1978).

Gunther, V. (1982). A Comparison of Bilingual Oral Language Reading Skills Among Limited English Speaking Children From Spanish-Speaking Backgrounds. In *Outstanding Dissertations in Bilingual Education, 1981.* Rosslyn, VA: National Clearinghouse for Bilingual Education.

Hakuta, K. (1986). *Mirror of Language: The Debate on Bilingualism.* New York: Basic Books.

Hakuta, K. (1975). Learning to Speak a Second Language: What Exactly Does the Child Learn? In D.P. Dato (Ed.), *Georgetown University Round Table on Languages and Linguistics.* Washington, D.C.: Georgetown University Press.

Hakuta, K. (1974). A Preliminary Report on the Development of Grammatical Morphemes in a Japanese Girl Learning English as a Second Language. *Working Papers in Bilingualism.* Toronto: The Ontario Institute for Studies in Education, 3, 18-43.

Hakuta, K., and Cancino. (1977). Trends in Second Language Acquisition Research. *Harvard Educational Review,* 47, 3, 294-316.

Hakuta, K., and Snow, C. (1986, January). The Role of Research in Policy Decisions About Bilingual Education. Washington, D.C.: U.S. House of Representatives, Education and Labor Committee.

Halcon, J. (1981). Features of Federal Bilingual Education Programs. *NABE Journal,* 6, (1), 27-39.

Halliday, M. (1975). Learning How to Mean: Explorations in the Development of Language. London: Dover Publications.

Hammerly, H. (1985). *An Integrated Theory of Language Teaching.* Burnby, Canada: Second Language Publications.

Hatch, E. (1974). Second Language Learning—Universal? *Working Papers on Bilingualism.* Toronto: The Ontario Institute for Studies in Education, 3, 1-16.

Hayes, Cherly D. (Ed.). (1982). *Making Policies for Children: A Study of the Federal Process.* Washington, D.C.: National Academy Press.

Hernandez-Chavez, E. (1984). The Inadequacy of English Immersion Education as an Educational Approach for Language Minority Students in the United States. In California State Department of Education (Ed.), *Studies on Immersion Education: A Collection for Educators.* Sacramento, CA: California State Department of Education. *NABE Journal,* 6, (1), 27-39.

Huerta, A. (1977, June). The Development of Codeswitching in a Young Bilingual. *Working Papers in Sociolinguistics*, No. 21.

Hymes, D. (1974). *Foundations in Sociolinguistics: An Ethnographic Approach.* Philadelphia: University of Pennsylvania.

Ianco-Worall, A. (1972). Bilingualism and Cognitive Development. *Child Development*, 43, 1390-1400.

Jacobs, J.F., and Pierce, M.L. (1966). Bilingualism and Creativity. *Elementary English*, 43, 499-503.

Juarez and Associates. (1981, November). *An Evaluation of the Head Start Bilingual Bicultural Curriculum Models, Executive Summary.* Washington, D.C.: Head Start Bureau, Office of Human Development Services, U.S. Department of Health and Human Services.

Judd, E.L. (1978). Factors Affecting the Passage of the Bilingual Education Act of 1967. Doctoral dissertation, New York University. Ann Arbor, Michigan: University Microfilm International.

Klein, D. (1980). Expressive and Referential Communication in Children's Early Language Development: The Relationship of Mothers' Communicative Styles. Ph.D. Dissertation, Michigan State University.

Kozolchyk, B. (1977). Toward a Theory on Law in Economic Development: The Costa Rican USAID-ROCAP Law Reform Project. *Arizona State Law Journal*, 681, 687.

Krashen, S.D. (1981). Bilingual Education and Second Language Acquisition Theory. In California State Department of Education (Ed.), *Schooling and Language Minority Students: A Theoretical Framework.* Los Angeles, CA: Evaluation, Dissemination and Assessment Center, California State University, Los Angeles, pp. 3-50.

Krashen, S.D. (1981). The Fundamental Pedagogical Principals in Second Language Teaching. *Studia Linguistica*, 35, (1-2), 51-71.

Krashen, S.D. (1982). *Principles and Practices in Second Language Acquisition.* Oxford: Pergamon.

Lambert, W.E., and Tucker, G.R. (1972). *Bilingual Education of Children: The St. Lambert Experiment.* Rowley, MA: Newbury House.

Lambert, W.E. (1967). A Social Psychology of Bilingualism. *Journal of Social Issues*, 23, (3), 91-109.

Lambert, W.E. and Peal, E. (1962). The Relationship of Bilingualism to Intelligence. *Psychological Monographs*, 76, 1-23.

Larsen-Freeman, D. (1976). An Explanation of the Morpheme Acquisition Order of Second Language Learners. *Language Learning*, 26, 125-134.

Lau vs. Nichols (1974). U.S. Supreme Court, 414 U.S. 563.

Leibowitz, A.H. (1982). *Federal Recognition of the Rights of Minority Language Groups.* Rosslyn, VA: National Clearinghouse for Bilingual Education.

Leibowitz, A.H. (1980). *The Bilingual Education Act: A Legislative Analysis.* Rosslyn, VA: National Clearinghouse for Bilingual Education.

Leibowitz, A.H. (1970). *Educational Policy and Political Acceptance: The Imposition of English as the Language of Instruction in American Schools.* Washington, D.C.: Center for Applied Linguistics.

Lenneberg, E.H., and Lenneberg, E. (1975). *Foundations of Language Development: Volume I and II*. London: UNESCO Press.

Leopold, W.F. (1939). *Speech Development of a Bilingual Child: A Linguist's Record Vol. I, Vocabulary Growth in the First Two Years*. Evanston, IL: Northwestern University Press.

Leopold, W.F. (1947). *Speech Development of a Bilingual Child: A Linguist's Record Vol. II, Sound Learning in the First Two Years*. Evanston, IL: Northwestern University Press.

Leopold, W.F. (1947a). *Speech Development of a Bilingual Child: A Linguist's Record Vol. III, Grammars and General Problems in the First Two Years*. Evanston, IL: Northwestern University Press.

Leopold, W.F. (1949b). *Speech Development of a Bilingual Child: A Linguist's Record, Vol. IV, Diary from Age Two*. Evanston, IL: Northwestern University Press.

Lerea, L., and Kohut, S. (1961). A Comparative Study of Monolinguals and Bilinguals in Verbal Task Performance. *Journal of Clinical Psychology*, 27, 49-52.

Lewis, H.P., and Lewis, E.R. (1965). Written Language Performance of Sixth-Grade Children of Low Socio-Economic Status from Bilingual and from Monolingual Backgrounds. *Journal of Experimental Education*, 35, 237-242.

Massachusetts Department of Education Bureau of Equal Educational Opportunity. (1986). *Seeking Educational Equity for Linguistic Minority Students*. Boston, MA: Massachusetts Department of Education. (Publication #14434-54-200-5-86.)

McLaughlin, B. (1978). *Second Language Acquisition in Childhood*. Hillsdale, NJ: Lawrence Erlbaum.

McLaughlin, B. (1984). *Second Language Acquisition in Childhood: Vol. 1: Preschool Children*. Hillsdale, NJ: Lawrence Erlbaum.

McLaughlin, B. (1985). *Second Language Acquisition in Childhood, Vol. 2: School-Age Children*. Hillsdale, New Jersey: Lawrence Erlbaum.

Menyuk, P. (1971). *The Acquisition and Development of Language*. Englewood Cliffs, NJ: Prentice-Hall.

Merino, B.J., and Politzer, R. (1977). *Toward Validation of Tests for Teachers in Spanish/English Bilingual Education Programs*. Research and Development Memorandum No. 151. Stanford Center for Research and Development in Teaching. Stanford University. (ED 143 708).

Michigan Department of Education. (1982). *First Evaluation of Bilingual Education Instruction Programs Administered in Michigan, 1979-1980 school year*. March.

Mr. Bennet and bilingual education. *Christian Science Monitor*, Sept. 30, 1985.

National Assessment of Educational Progress. (1986). *Literacy: Profiles of America's Young Adults*. Princeton, NJ: Educational Testing Services.

National Institute of Education. (1981). *Report of the National Institute of Education on the Testing and Assessment Implications of the Title VI Language Minority Proposed Rules*. Washington, D.C.: National Institute of Education.

O'Malley, J.M. (1982). Instructional Services for Limited English Proficient Children. *NABE Journal*, 7, 1, 14-36.

O'Malley, J.M. (1981). *Children's and Services Study: Language Minority Children with Limited English Proficiency in the United States*. Rosslyn, VA: National Clearinghouse for Bilingual Education.

O'Malley, J.M. (1978). Review of the Evaluation of the Impact of ESEA Title VII Spanish-English Bilingual Education Programs. *Bilingual Resources*, 1, (2), 6-10.

Orenstein, M. (1987, April). Official English Battle Widens. *Hispanic Link Weekly Report*, 5, 16, 1-2.

Orum, Lori (1984). *The Bilingual Education Act of 1984: Community Involvement in Policy Development*. Mimeographed report. Washington, D.C.: National Council of La Raza.

Pacheco, M.T. (1973). Approaches to Bilingualism: Recognition of a Multilingual Society. In D.C. Langue (Ed.), *Pluralism in Foreign Language Education*. Skokie, IL: National Textbook, Inc.

Padilla, A.M., and Liebman, E. (1975). Language Acquisition in the Bilingual Child. *The Bilingual Review/La Revista Bilingüe*, 2, 34-55.

Pavlovitch, M. (1920). *Le Language Enfantin: Acquisition du Ferbe et du Francais par un Enfant Serbe*. Paris: Champion.

Peal, E., and Lambert, W.E. (1962). The Relation of Bilingualism to Intelligence. *Psychological Monographs: General and Applied*, 76, 546, 1-23.

Peck, S. (1978). Child-Child Discourse in Second Language Acquisition. In E. Hatch (Ed.), *Second Language Acquisition*. Rowley, MA: Newbury House, 118-137.

Phillips, S.U. (1972). Participant Structures and Communication Incompetence: Warm Springs Children in Community and Classroom. In C. Cazden, D. Hymes and W.J. John (Eds.), *Function of a Language in the Classroom*. New York: Teachers College Press.

Phillips, S.U. (1983). *The Invisible Culture*. New York: Longman.

Ramirez, A., and Stromquist, N. (1979). ESL Methodology and Student Learning in Bilingual Elementary School. *TESOL Quarterly*, 13, 145-158.

Ramirez, A. (1985). *Bilingualism Through Schooling*. Albany, NY: State University of New York Press.

Ramirez, D., Merino, B., Bye, T., and Gold, N. (1982). Assessment of Oral English Proficiency: A Status Report. Paper presented at the Fifth International Symposium of Educational Testing, University of Stilling, Scotland.

Ramirez, J.D. (1986). Comparing Structured English Immersion and Bilingual Education: First Year Results of a National Study. *American Journal of Education*, 95, 1, 122-148.

Richards, J., and Rodgers, T.S. (1986). *Approaches and Methods in Language Teaching*. Cambridge: Cambridge University Press.

Ronjat, S.V. (1913). *Le Development du Language Ovserve Chez un Enfant Bilingue*. Paris: Champion.

Roos, P. (1984, July). Legal Guidelines for Bilingual Administrators. Invited address, Society for Research in Child Development. Austin, TX.

Rosansky, E. (1979). A Review of the Bilingual Syntax Measure. In Spolsky (Ed.), *Advances in Language Testing Series: I*. Arlington, VA: Center for Applied Linguistics.

Rosenthal, A., Milne, A., Ginsburg, A., and Baker, K. (1981). *A Comparison of the Effects of Language Background and Socioeconomic Status on Achievement Among Elementary School Students*. Washington, D.C.: System Development Corporation to the U.S. Department of Education under Contract No. 300-75-0332.

Rosier, P., and Holm, W. (1980). The Rock Point Experience: A Longitudinal Study of a Navajo School Program (Saad Naaki Bee Na'nitin). *Bilingual Education Series 8: Papers in Applied Linguistics*. Arlington, VA: Center for Applied Linguistics. (ED 195 363).

Rosier, P.A. (1977). Comparative Study of Two Approaches of Introducing Initial Reading to Navajo Children: The Direct Method and the Native Language Method. Ph.D. Dissertation, Northern Arizona University.

Rotberg, I. (1982). Some Legal and Research Considerations in Establishing Federal Policy in Bilingual Education. *Harvard Education Review*, 52, 2, 149-168.

S.R.A. Technologies, Inc. (1984). *Descriptive Analysis of Title VII — Funded State Education Agency Activities*. Report submitted to the U.S. Department of Education (#7706-83-4690).

Schneider, S.G. (1976). *Revolution, Reaction or Reform: The 1974 Bilingual Education Act*. New York: Las Americas.

Schumann, J.H. (1976). Affective Factors and the Problem of Age in Second Language Acquisition. *Language Learning*, 25, 209-239.

Seliger, H.W. (1984). Processing Universals in Second Language Acquisition. In F.R. Eckman, L.H. Bell, and D. Nelson (Eds.), *Universals of Second Language Acquisition*. Rowley, MA: Newbury House, 161-183.

Seliger, H.W. (1977). Does Practice Make Perfect? A Study of Interactional Patterns and L2 Competence. *Language Learning*, 27, 2, 263-278.

Shantz, C. (1977). The Development of Social Cognition. In E.M. Hetherington (Ed.), *Review of Child Development Research* (Vol. 5). Chicago, IL: University of Chicago Press.

Skinner, B.J. (1957). *Verbal Behavior*. Englewood Cliffs, NJ: Prentice-Hall.

Skozylas, R.V. (1977). An Evaluation of Some Cognitive and Affective Aspects of a Spanish-English Bilingual Program. Ph.D. Dissertation, The University of New Mexico.

Skrabanek, R.L. (1970). Language Maintenance Among Mexican-Americans. *International Journal of Comparative Sociology*, 11, 272-282.

Smith, M.D. (1935). A Study of the Speech of Eight Bilingual Children of the Same Family. *Child Development*, 6, 19-25.

So, A., and Chan, K. (1984). What Matters? The Relative Impact of Language Background and Socioeconomic Status on Reading Achievement. *NABE Journal VII*, (3), 27-40.

Sorenson, A.P. (1967). Multilingualism in the Northwest Amazon. *American Anthropologist*, 69, 67-68.

Stein, Colman (1986). *Sink or Swim: The Politics of Bilingual Education*. New York: Praeger.

Steinberg, L., Blinde, P.L., and Chan, K.S. (1984). Dropping Out Among Language-Minority Youth. *Review of Educational Research*, 54(1):113-132.

Swain, M., and Lapkin, S. (1982). *Evaluating Bilingual Education: A Canadian Case Study*. Clevedon/Avon, England: Multicultural Matters.

Tempes, F. (1985). *Case Studies in Bilingual Education*. California State Department of Education Bilingual Education Office. First Year Report (federal grant #G008303723).

Thonis, E. (1981). Reading Instruction for Language Minority Students. In California State Department of Education (Ed.), *Schooling and Language Minority Students: A Theoretical Framework*. Los Angeles: Evaluation and Dissemination and Assessment Center, California State University, Los Angeles.

Tikenoff, W.J. (1983). *Compatibility of the SBIF Features with Other Research on Instruction of LEP Students*. San Francisco, California: Far West Laboratory (SBIF-83-4.8/10).

Tikenoff, W.J. (September, 1983). *Significant Bilingual Instructional Features Study*. San Francisco, CA: Far West Laboratory.

Troike, R. (1978). *Research Evidence for the Effectiveness of Bilingual Education*. Roslyn, VA: National Clearinghouse for Bilingual Education.

U.S. Department of Commerce—Census. (1975). *Special Studies: Language Usage in the United States: July 1975*. Washington, D.C.: U.S. Government Printing Office.

U.S. Department of Education, National Clearinghouse for Bilingual Education. (1986). *Forum, IX*, 3.

U.S. Department of Education, National Clearinghouse for Bilingual Education. (1985). *State Education Agency Information 1984-85*. Rosslyn, VA: National Clearinghouse for Bilingual Education.

U.S. Department of Education. (1984). Estimates and Characteristics of Teachers for Elementary and Secondary Programs and Services for Language Minority Limited English Proficient Students. *The Condition of Bilingual Education in the Nation*. Washington, D.C.: U.S. Department of Education.

U.S. General Accounting Office. (1987, March). *Research Evidence on Bilingual Education*. Washington, D.C.: U.S. General Accounting Office, GAO/PEMD-87-12BR.

Ulibarri, D.M., Spencer, M.L., and Rivas, G.A. (1981). Language Proficiency and Academic Achievement: A Study of Language Proficiency Tests and Their Relationship to School Ratings as Predictions of Academic Achievement. *NABE Journal*, 5, 3, 47-80.

Waggoner, D. (1978). Geographic Distribution, Nativity, and Age Distribution of Language Minorities in the U.S., Spring 1976. *NCES Bulletin*, 78-B, No. 5. U.S. Department of Education, National Center for Education Statistics. Washington, D.C.

Waggoner, D. (1984). The Need for Bilingual Education: Estimates from the 1980 Census. *NABE Journal*, 8, 1-14.

Willig, A.C. (1985). A Meta-Analysis of Selected Studies on the Effectiveness of Bilingual Education. *Review of Educational Research*, 55, 269-317.

Winters, W., de Porcel, A., and Nadeau, A. (1982). Reclassification of Bilingual Program Participants: A System and Four Perspectives—Curriculum, Research, Instruction, and Evaluation. Paper presented at the California Educational Research Association. Sacramento, CA.

Wong-Fillmore, L., Ammon, P., McLaughlin, B., and Ammon, M.S. (1985). Learning English Through Bilingual Instruction (BIE #400-360-0030). Rosslyn, Virginia: National Clearinghouse for Bilingual Education.

Wong-Fillmore, L. (1976). The Second Time Around: Cognitive and Social Strategies in Second Language Acquisition. Ph.D. Dissertation, Stanford University.

Yates, J.R., and Ortiz, A.A. (1983). Baker-DeKanter Review: Inappropriate Conclusions on the Efficacy of Bilingual Education. *NABE Journal*, 7, 3, 75-84.

Zentella, A.C. (1981). Ta Bien You Could Answer me en Cualquier Idioma: Puerto Rican Codeswitching in Bilingual Classrooms. In R. Duran (Ed.), *Latino Language and Communicative Behavior*. Norwood, NJ: Ablex Publishing Corp., 109-132.

INDEX

135